Funny Business

Funny Business

Moguls, Mobsters, Megastars, and the Mad, Mad World of the Ad Game

ALLEN ROSENSHINE

B
Beaufort Books
New York

ISBN 10: 0-8253-0539-X
ISBN 13: 978-0-8253-0539-9

Published in the United States by Beaufort Books, New York
Distributed by Midpoint Trade Books, New York
www.midpointtradebooks.com

2 4 6 8 10 9 7 5 3 1

PRINTED IN THE UNITED STATES OF AMERICA

For Anna, Missy, Anita,
Andy, Jon, Lizzy, and Laura,
who too often bore the brunt of my frustration
when the business wasn't so funny.

Contents

Foreword

Despite my more than forty years at BBDO, one of the world's largest advertising agencies, this is not a "how-to" book on advertising. It's not about policies, procedures, or process. Rather, it's a collection of stories that happened *in* advertising. It's about people with whom I worked and all kinds of off-the-wall, or at least off-the-beaten-path, events in the business.

It's about clients, many of them anointed — and some self-appointed — moguls in the business world. It's about the occasional members of the underworld — mobsters whom we sometimes had to deal with in order to get our work done. It's about famous personalities from entertainment, sports, and politics — often megastars who endorsed and promoted our clients' products. It's about the wackiness of the advertising business and sometimes of the business world in general, which is the case far more often than you might imagine.

Some of my friends and colleagues have urged me to write something instructional or inspirational, or to advance a point of view about the future of the business, or to present a rationale supporting the importance of what we do. Frankly, I much more enjoy telling stories I think are funny, because at the end of the day, compared to most vocations, advertising just doesn't rank as a serious business. It's not called "the ad *game*" for nothing.

I remember being a young nervous wreck moments before the top management of the agency would enter the BBDO boardroom to review the status of one of the accounts for which I wrote ads and commercials. I had just recently joined the agency and was not exactly feeling as though the advertising world was my oyster. The account executive, noticing my neurotic state, shook his head, smiling.

"Calm down, Allen," he said. "It's just a game."

In time, I came to realize that no matter how many hundreds of billions of dollars are spent on advertising every year, and regardless of how seriously some people who run agencies may take themselves, there is at least as much lunacy as logic where Madison Avenue crosses the streets of the corporate world.

These stories are living proof.

But in no way do they deny the incredibly hard work, the mind-opening creativity, the dedication and commitment to insight and innovation, and the significant contributions to commerce that I have seen in the advertising world.

Many others have chronicled how advertising works, what it takes to do it well, who are its best practitioners, why it is critical to entrepreneurial competition and the healthy growth of free market economies, and so on. Among them is my colleague at BBDO for nearly three decades, Phil Dusenberry, in his recent book, *Then We Set His Hair on Fire.* As earnest as Phil's book is, his title nonetheless headlines a world quite different, to say the least, from most other businesses.

When they meet, it is often a face-off between the largely left-brain world of business and the predominantly right-brain practice of advertising.

Left-brain thinking is ostensibly (I suppose I should do this alphabetically) coherent, consistent, logical, methodical, objective, orderly, rational, reasonable, sequential, and systematic. Theoretically, the right side of the brain governs (this time in appropriately random order) our creative, intuitive, subjective, emotional, artistic, indiscriminate, aesthetic, and spontaneous inclinations. According to these widely accepted beliefs, most of us behave more under the influence of one side of our brains than the other.

So when you hear someone described as a businessman or businesswoman, you might expect that the left side of the brain dominates his or her thinking. The world of manufacturing and more recently, the newer world of information — both affected by the developing phenomenon of globalization — are typified by their growing need for organization, finance, technology, and a host of complicated relationships between many more specific and relatively objective disciplines. In business school, you study economics, accounting, marketing, corporate strategy, management, labor relations, and the like, along with the logistics of producing, distributing, and ultimately selling goods or services at a profit throughout more and more of the world. You won't find too many courses in art, music, drama, literature, poetry, or philosophy in the MBA curriculum.

And while you will encounter people with business degrees in advertising, a far greater force in agencies comes from the right brains of the writers, art directors, and designers of traditional as well as new technology communications — in short, the creative people and the consumer psychologists who guide their efforts. Advertising defies the norms of business by arguably leaning well to the right side of the brain. Thus, one of the most perceptive and often quoted comments about advertising from John Wanamaker, the department store developer, who said he knew half his advertising was a waste of money, but he didn't know *which* half.

You can see recent dramatic proof of the disarray and devastation that can occur when these two diametrically different dimensions of the human mind come into conflict. Consider the period in the mid-to-late 1990s when dotcom companies driven by the Internet were started and run mostly by right-brain thinkers. The dotcom bubble is what ultimately happened in business when the right brains — aided and abetted by advisors and advocates with *no* brains — took over from the left brains. When the bubble inevitably burst, it blew up in the faces of practically everyone, even people who should have known better. Lou Dobbs, then the CNN guru of business, told me in 1999, when the Dow Jones Industrial Average had climbed past 10,000, that he saw no reason why it would not continue its surge beyond 12,000 within that very year. A few months later, he left CNN to start his own dotcom, no doubt with some intention of cashing in on the craze. Six *years* later, after its precipitous plunge, the Dow was finally back where it had been. And so was Lou. But while he may have suffered mostly from embarrassment, millions of others were left in financial ruins.

Admittedly, there was nothing funny about this right-brain collision with the left-brain world of business. But that destructive episode aside, funny things very often do happen, none more than from the mix of advertising and big business. That's what these stories are about — the laughable or ironic or just curious things that have happened to me and people I've known over the past four decades.

The capriciousness of the advertising business makes it a breeding ground for unusual if not unstable characters. It's an almost daily exhibition of madcap behavior. It's a haven for people trained for other kinds of work, but who failed at, or became bored with, whatever they had studied to do. It's populated by the highly educated as well as the questionably literate. In any meeting, you might hear wonderfully creative ideas from people who are bright, intuitive, witty, and clever, alternating with incoherent blather from others with little or no idea what they're talking about. It's replete with personalities hobbled by their continuous conflict between sometimes justified egomania and ever-present insecurity, riding an emotional rollercoaster where success or failure is determined by people and events beyond their control.

If it sounds something like Hollywood, that's because the entertainment business is another major enterprise in which right-brain thinking dominates. It's surely debatable as to which business is crazier. But unlike Hollywood, advertising is far less driven by money, power, or fame. Of course, you can make good money in advertising, but top executives and stars in Hollywood earn considerably more. You have very little power in advertising, since in almost all cases, the clients call the shots and they can replace an agency at the drop of a sales curve. As for fame, how many people outside advertising have ever heard of anyone in it? If you're neither in the business nor a client, my name will no doubt come as news to you, unless we're related or one of us owes the other money.

In any event, I'd argue that advertising people are considerably more humane and surely more real, at least physically, than the folks in Tinseltown. Most of the hair, noses, eyes, chins, breasts, stomachs, buttocks, thighs, and other body parts in advertising have not been surgically altered. And mentally, we probably don't become as detached from reality by living in a fishbowl, constantly exposed to and judged by a frenzied press and fickle public.

At the end of the day, when you work in advertising, you get to live quite a few right-brain moments in business. These stories are some of them. They're about actual events I either took part in or were told to me. I couldn't make up stuff like this, although admittedly I've taken the liberty of recreating dialogue and adding some embellishment here and there for emphasis. As in the advertising I've written, the speeches I've given, or the presentations I've made to clients over the years, I'm not above using a little exaggeration once in a while to make a point.

As for the people involved, in almost all cases I'm using their real names. Infrequently, there's an admitted pseudonym if the situation might hurt or embarrass someone. It's not that I'm trying to show how considerate I am. It's just that I don't have enough years left to make new friends or waste time with lawyers. The only other exceptions are a few stories in which it's *my* well-being I'm worried about. Using the actual names of certain people in these cases wouldn't particularly harm *them*. It would, however, likely cause severe damage to my health, starting with my kneecaps.

So these stories are not really about advertising per se. They're not about the rules or strategies or scoring of the game, but more about the people who play it, and their unconventional dealings with the world of business. From logic run amuck, to the corporate equivalent of a vaudeville pratfall, many experiences over the years have left me scratching my head or laughing out loud.

Advertising can be nerve wracking, ego wrenching, personality warping, family breaking, and in many other ways, life altering. It's not the easiest business. But it is a *funny* business.

That's the part I'd like to share with you.

Funny Business

Kiss Your Hemorrhoids Goodbye

Before I joined BBDO in 1965, I worked for almost three years at a small advertising agency. It was my first job in the business. I had finished college and had taken the agency job for just one reason—the only other offer I had was from a publishing company for twenty-five dollars a week less.

So much for career planning.

The clients were all industrial manufacturers as opposed to companies that market everyday consumers products. They never advertised on television. Their customers were typically other businesses not requiring mass media to reach them. Television is not particularly conducive to selling conveyor belts, concrete, and other construction materials, so after a couple of years writing catalogs, brochures, and an occasional magazine ad, I had still never done a TV commercial.

It seemed a good idea to at least take a course in creating television advertising, which I did during evenings after work. The class consisted of me, a few other advertising wannabes, and some obviously bored housewives looking for something supposedly amusing to do. It was taught by an advertising executive from the Ted Bates company, a large advertising firm known for its "hard sell" commercials, mostly for household products that cleaned everything from teeth to toilets, and pharmaceuticals for relieving a variety of aches, pains, clogs, itches, wheezes, and sneezes.

This was not the kind of advertising my classmates and I had in mind when we signed up for the course. We were hoping to learn about sexy, humorous beer commercials or the fun and games of soft-drink advertising. But our products would be remedies for hammers in the head, sickness in the stomach, bacteria in the bathroom, or as it turned out one evening, pains in the posterior. It was on this subject that one of the women took our teacher to task.

"Why do you guys do those disgusting hemorrhoid commercials?" she asked.

"Well it's true that Preparation H is one of our clients," he answered with a patient and knowing smile, "so let me explain how the advertising works."

"Those shitty commercials *work*?" she retorted, the pun not lost on the laughing class.

"Oh yes, and here's why," said our professor of pain relief. "A commercial for Preparation H is seen by about fifty million people. Forty-five million of them are probably like you," he said, pointing at her. "They don't have hemorrhoids and they don't like watching our advertising. But the other five million do have the problem. And of those," he went on, warming to his subject, "maybe twenty percent, say about a million of them, are suffering from pain and itching at the very moment they see the commercial. So you can bet they're paying attention. And if just half of those, let's say about five hundred thousand people, are convinced by our commercial that Preparation H can relieve their problem, we've got a sales success and a happy client on our hands. So," he concluded on a note of triumph, "we don't really give a damn if you and the other forty-nine million, five hundred thousand people don't like our commercial!"

I should have known right then what I was in for.

It should have been obvious that any business that could

2

boast of success even when it failed ninety-nine percent of the time—and turned most people off—would have a large quotient of craziness.

But like most people in advertising, even had I known, I would have had no idea what else to do with myself.

I think that explains a lot.

Angelo's Secret

About half a life ago, as I began to live the cliché of climbing the corporate ladder, I would occasionally treat myself to a shoeshine in my office at BBDO. Actually, I didn't have a real office with four walls and a door. I worked in one of the many cubicles that in most companies occupy the open floor area inside the perimeter of window offices. My boss had one of those, befitting his corporate rank.

Every day, a guy named Angelo would go from office to office, shining shoes. One time, Angelo came to my boss's office while I was there showing him some work. My boss introduced me to Angelo and paid for me to have a shine. Then, adding to his magnanimous gesture, he said to Angelo that he shouldn't ignore me just because I didn't have an office, clearly implying Angelo might shine my shoes even though I worked in one of the lower-class cubicles. He made a point of telling Angelo that I was an up-and-coming writer, thus granting me my first status symbol as one worthy of Angelo's attention.

So whenever I had trouble coming up with an idea for an ad or commercial, which usually caused a precipitous drop in my self-confidence, having Angelo shine my shoes always reminded me of my boss's good opinion. But at the end of every shine, as he snapped his buffing rag back and forth across my

4

shoes, he always offered a subtle reminder that he had lowered himself to working in a poorer neighborhood.

"Hey, you gonna get an office soon?" he'd look up and ask.

"I don't know, Angelo," I'd reply. "What d' you hear?"

"Hey, your boss, he likes you," he'd say, completing the ritual of leaving me with shinier shoes and a renewed belief in a brighter future.

Some months later, my boss called me into his office, telling me to shut the door. That could have meant any number of things, including my being out of a job in the next few minutes. However, having only recently had some of my work actually appear in the media, and having heard again that very morning Angelo's assurance of my boss's approval, optimism outweighed the paranoia that usually grips advertising people in response to anything unexpected. But the bright side quickly darkened as my boss slowly leaned forward from behind his desk, his face more grim than I'd ever seen it.

Uh, oh, Angelo's wrong, I thought. *I'm getting canned.*

"If you say one word of what I'm about to tell you," said my boss through clenched teeth, "I'll fire your ass so fast, the rest of you will be chasing it out the door."

I didn't really know how to respond but I felt it necessary to offer an immediate pledge of allegiance. I answered in no uncertain terms.

"My lips are sealed," I swore.

He seemed momentarily taken aback, probably thinking that the boldness and wit of his threat deserved a less inane response from a writer whose work he praised and supported. But he quickly recovered and dropped his bomb.

"I'm leaving BBDO," he announced. "I'm outta here, so you should think about who you wanna work for. I'm letting you know now, so you don't get caught by surprise later when I talk to them upstairs. But I'm warning you, if one word about this gets out, I'll know it was you, 'cause you're the only one I'm telling."

Now I really didn't know what to say. But I wasn't going to let myself lapse into another cliché.

"Wow!" I exclaimed.

After another quizzical look, he continued.

"So if you wanna know what happened," he said, "I'm not telling you, 'cause it's personal. But I'm warning you again, not a word to anybody. If anyone finds out about this, I'll deny it and fire you for starting a rumor that I'm leaving."

As I left his office, I didn't know what to think. I knew enough to appreciate the confidence my boss had shown in me, and that he had done me a big favor by telling me, and not anyone else, about his departure. Beyond that, I only knew for sure that what I knew could get me fired.

After a mostly sleepless night, I sat at my desk the next morning, trying to figure out my next step. Then Angelo stuck his head around the opening in the partition of my cubicle.

"Hey, you wanna shine?"

My mind was a mess, but there was no reason my shoes should be too, so I waved him in. A few minutes later, as he finished, he looked up, and I thought about how, in the light of yesterday's news, I should answer his usual question about when I would get an office. I didn't have to think for long.

"Hey," he said, "I hear your boss is quittin'. Now you gonna get an office f' sure!"

"What?" I shouted, seeing the pink slip before my eyes. "Where the hell did you hear he's leaving?"

"Hey, he just tol' me. But ya gotta keep it down," Angelo whispered. "He said nobody else knew, an' if I say anythin', he's gonna fire me."

A few weeks later, my boss left. And Angelo gave me my first shoeshine in my new office.

Getting a Grip on AT&T

The first television commercial I ever worked on was for New York Telephone, which ultimately was consolidated within AT&T as part of a restructuring of the industry. The assignment was simple, straightforward, and not very exciting — the perfect training ground for a novice copywriter.

The objective was to alert people who were moving that they needed to arrange for their new phone service a few months in advance, if they wanted to be connected on the day they actually moved. I am fairly certain that this rather excessive requirement was a result of the fact that at the time, the phone company enjoyed the power and prerogatives of a monopoly, not required to compete for customers by offering anything approximating accommodating service. Being the only game in town, they set the rules, and consumers had little choice but to live by them.

It was not surprising, therefore, that the attitude of the phone company management was typified by the arrogance of the unchallenged. They ruled their company, their suppliers, and the public with an iron hand and the mindlessness of an automaton governed by processes and procedures that would not permit any deviation regardless of its potential merit. They had somewhere between little and no tolerance for any new idea that might require adaptation or adjustment of their etched-in-stone methodologies. They didn't much care what their customers thought and they cared even less about the opinions of their advertising agency.

Our people lived in constant fear of their displeasure, not only because that is the inherent nature of the relationship between agencies and their clients, but also for the more practical reason that if we lost their business, there was no other local phone company to replace them.

This was the mission and the milieu in which I would bring to bear all the powers of sight, sound, language, motion, drama, and creativity to craft a memorable and persuasive message delivered in thirty seconds. But given the nature of the client, the fear and trembling they engendered among our agency account executives, and my own inexperience with the genre, I reckoned that this was no time for me to break new ground in television advertising.

I devised a script of such obvious simplicity, such uncontroversial sincerity, such unabashed unpretentiousness, a scene so extraordinarily insipid as to delight my agency colleagues and earn a grim nod of approval from our client. The commercial would open on a couple — young, white, and without even the slightest hint of New York's melting-pot ethnicity — entering their new apartment filled with unopened boxes and unarranged furniture, clearly at the moment of moving in. But amid this chaos, one object of normalcy, one beacon of contact with the best of all possible worlds of order and stability sat prominently on the floor — their newly installed telephone. It was there, as the announcer knowingly intoned, because they had the foresight and vision to have ordered it in the timely manner dictated by New York Telephone. Had they failed to do so, the voice of the company gravely observed, they would have been unable to reach whomever the young man was now happily dialing.

It was at this climactic moment during the filming of the

8

commercial that everything suddenly began to unravel. As the camera rolled to capture the moment the actor dialed his first number on his new phone, the client leaped from his chair.

"*Stop!* Stop the camera! Stop everything!" he shouted.

Even the urgency of his order didn't completely convey the seriousness of the moment. Since this was my first commercial production, I didn't immediately realize the enormous breach of etiquette, along with the violation of various union rules, that had just occurred. No one could give orders to the film crew except the director. Everyone on the set was stunned, no one more so than our account executive, who was responsible for guaranteeing that the client's comfort, wishes, and concerns were totally attended to.

"*What?*" he gasped. "What happened? What's the problem?"

"The problem," replied the client, imitating our account man and fixing his furious stare on the actor, "is him."

"I don't understand," our account man answered. "He's dialing a number just like the script says. What is he doing wrong?" he asked, his tone somewhere between a whimper and a whine.

The client turned from the actor and looked at our account executive with an expression of utter disbelief mixed with clear contempt.

"What he is doing wrong," he mimicked, "is that he is out of compliance with the established procedures of the New York Telephone Company, which you and your company," he added threateningly, "ought to be well aware of."

Having been the creator of this moment of apparent disaster and being only a writer who would not necessarily be expected to know, much less understand, the intricacies of the client's operations, I thought I might take advantage of my assumed ignorance to clarify the issue. And seeing the sweat that had broken out on my colleague's beaten brow, I wasn't sure he was capable of even the obvious next question.

"If you can tell me what you don't want the actor to do," I said, "I'm sure we can revise the script."

"What I don't want the actor to do," he replied, this time mocking me, "is to hold the phone receiver in a blatantly unauthorized manner."

I looked at the actor, who hadn't moved an inch during these exchanges, still with the receiver at his ear.

"How should he hold it?" I asked, in a tone as measured as I could muster to avoid conveying the incredulity I actually felt.

"The receiver of a telephone is held with the thumb and all four fingers of the hand wrapped around the center of the stem, equidistant between the earpiece and the speaker. It is never, ever, held *that* way," he said, tossing a glance at the petrified actor, "with the finger extended along the length of the receiver."

At this moment, our account man emerged from his catatonic state.

"Of course! Yes, now I see it!" he exclaimed. And with that, he pointed at the actor, exclaiming, "You heard the client. Hold the phone *properly*!"

The client returned to his seat with a look of triumph. Our account executive collapsed, more than sat down, in his chair. The actor continued to stand frozen in place.

The director, who all the while had stood by just looking back and forth between the client, our account man, and me without uttering a word despite his mouth hanging open in disbelief, finally reestablished command of the session.

"Okay," he said, now with the bored detachment of a cinematic artiste who would only lower himself to doing commercials as a way to pursue his dream of directing a Hollywood film, "let's get those fucking fingers around the fucking phone and get this fucking thing over with."

Nap Time

I'm sure that at one time or another, all people in business worry about falling asleep during a meeting. And I assume the extent of the concern would depend largely on the nature of the meeting and its attendees. For example, it would obviously be far worse to doze off in front of a client who pays for your ostensibly dedicated and observant attention, than to catch a few winks in a meeting strictly with associates from your own company. Although if they are people who can determine your compensation, responsibilities, title, or other forms of your corporate fate, I don't recommend it.

Less worrisome, but nonetheless a cause for concern in the business of creating advertising, is the occasion when the *client* nods off while you present your agency's recommendations for their next campaign. Of course, in that situation, you would not be guilty of embarrassing yourself. But it might just occur to you, as you deliver the usually impassioned presentation of how the advertising would look, along with the confident rationale for why it will work to persuade and motivate the consumer, that the closed eyes and drooping head of the client suggest your work is falling on ears deafened by boredom. For those whose creativity, intelligence, and sense of self-worth are on the line, a sleeping client can be a much

11

greater blow to the ego than one who just fails to applaud.

I know, because it happened to me twice — that is, putting a client to sleep, not just getting a negative reaction. (The latter happened many more times than I'm prepared to admit.)

On the first occasion, I was presenting ideas for a television campaign to the chief executive of a company for which we advertised a leading cosmetic product. I was somewhat on edge because I had never met him before and had not yet experienced many meetings with heads of our client companies. But because the presentation had already received approvals from the various levels of marketing staffs below him, I saw this as more of a formality to get the final go-ahead rather than a critical appraisal of our work. Owing to our success in the previous meetings, I was optimistic that this one, which included only the CEO in his office, would be equally positive.

And so, with our top executive on the account at my side, I began my performance.

I was concentrating so hard on describing the scenes and acting out the roles of the people in the first commercial of the new campaign, that I didn't pay too much attention to any initial reactions from the client. This was the most critical of the commercials because it would establish the idea of all the advertising to follow, and I was totally absorbed in explaining it. It wasn't until I had finished with a dramatic proclamation of the new slogan ending the commercial that I looked up to see the client, unmistakably *asleep*.

No, he wasn't momentarily closing his eyes to help visualize what I had described. And he wasn't in one of those few moments of diminished consciousness from which we snap quickly back to attention.

He was dead to the world.

I didn't know what to do next. Do I stop until he wakes up? I could have been there until the next morning. Do I continue my sales pitch in the hope that some of it might be absorbed subconsciously? Do I cough or sneeze or "accidentally" knock something off his desk so that he might react to the noise? I looked to my colleague for help, which he offered by silently nodding his head and waving the back of his hand to me in a signal to go on as though nothing was wrong.

Having no better idea of my own, that's what I did. I spent the next fifteen minutes describing ideas for what was intended to be many millions of dollars worth of advertising, not to mention *my* creative work, to Rip Van Winkle.

Fortunately, he didn't sleep quite as long. When I finished, the account man gestured to me to just sit back and relax. A minute or two later, the client awoke. Without the slightest allusion to what had happened, he told us that since his people had already approved the campaign, it was fine with him. He then thanked us for coming, we shook hands, and he showed us out.

The door had no sooner closed behind us when I blurted out, "What the hell happened in there?"

"Well, I guess I should have warned you beforehand," said the account guy, "but I've been told he's got narcolepsy. I've seen him fall asleep in meetings before."

I was still so shaken that it didn't even occur to me to ask how anyone managed to run a company under those circumstances. As it turned out, the answer would probably have been "Not very well," since he was replaced shortly thereafter.

I had quite a different reaction the second time a client fell asleep on me.

This time, I presented on my home turf, at BBDO. The client was a top executive at Gillette, one of the largest companies we served and one with which we had done business for decades. Our assignment was to develop a corporate campaign extolling the company's history of providing breakthrough new products resulting from their ongoing commitment to consumer research, technological innovation, and manufacturing precision. The campaign was the brainchild of this particular manager, who hoped to sell it to his board of directors as an example of his strategy to build the value of the Gillette brand among consumers and improve its share price on the stock market.

I thought we had created some really exceptional ads to communicate his message and I looked forward to the meeting in which I would present them. It took place in the office of the BBDO executive in charge of the Gillette account, with just the three of us present.

I began to show our work with great enthusiasm, and after explaining the first three of about ten ads, which included reading each ad's copy celebrating Gillette's product development excellence, I paused for some reaction and discussion. None was forthcoming. The client was *out cold,* his head tilted backward, his mouth open, his eyes shut to the world — my world of creativity going totally unnoticed.

I looked at our account executive, who just shrugged his shoulders as if to say he had no idea what we should do. I again thought of the "inadvertent noise ploy," but this time I found myself more annoyed than fearful that I and the work were somehow guilty of losing his attention. I decided to tailor my presentation to my snoozing audience.

"The next ad in our campaign," I said, "shows how the *fragamitz explacitor,* which Gillette scientists discovered while on their most recent trip to the rings of Saturn, enables a razor to shave without a man actually touching it, by virtue of the *omnisigalian refluxivation* effect."

I glanced from the face of the client to our account man, who had turned pale, his eyes as wide open as the client's were shut, violently shaking his head back and forth, and frantically waving his hands at me to stop. Since the client still showed no sign of consciousness, I was determined to go on.

"The *blah-blahvian regenerosis* highlighted in the copy of this ad," I continued, "positions Gillette at the forefront of companies currently employing the most advanced *catacli-*

matic symbiocrustavian technologies, supported by marketing executives who wouldn't know an Einsteinian *golamicinist* from a Freudian *contubist*."

By this point, our account executive looked like a mime in a state of silent apoplexy, which became total panic as I picked up a large glass ashtray from his desk and dropped it on the client's foot.

"Sorry," I said, as he woke with a start. "As you could see," I added with an ingratiating smile, "I got a little carried away explaining the last ad in the campaign. We're really excited about it and we hope you are as well," I concluded.

"Oh, that's okay," he replied, wincing as he handed me the ashtray. "I really can't tell you how much I like this work," he continued, not realizing the literal truth of his comment. "It's terrific and exactly what I was looking for."

I gathered up the ads for him, he put them in his briefcase, and we said our goodbyes. I added, "Sweet dreams," under my breath, and he left.

"Don't you ever pull a stunt like that again," the account guy exclaimed when the client was out of earshot. "What if he woke up?" he asked, still horrified.

"He did, and he loved the work, so what's the problem?" I said, laughing. "But you're right," I assured him, hoping that might have a calming effect on his agitation. "I'll never do that to him again," I promised.

And I didn't, because he was gone from Gillette shortly thereafter, likely having fallen asleep in front of someone for whom he wasn't the client — someone less tolerant, less understanding, and less forgiving than I.

Did Someone Order a Diet Coke?

As part of a television campaign for Diet Pepsi, we asked Lee Iacocca, then chairman and chief executive officer of Chrysler, to appear in one of our commercials. Lee, also a client of BBDO, and not normally averse to public appearances, agreed. He rightly believed that Chrysler's generally uninspiring image would benefit from a leader seen as a personality in the public eye. Diet Pepsi, in turn, would be shown at the lips of one of America's most admired businessmen.

On the evening before the filming, we hosted a dinner for Roger Enrico, head of Pepsi-Cola, to meet Lee. His fiancée, Peggy Johnson; Roger's wife, Rosemary; and my wife, Missy, joined us. Lee and Roger had much in common. Both were leaders in their respective businesses, both underdogs in their product categories fighting against bigger and stronger competition, but nevertheless enjoying success in the car and cola wars, and both proud of their Italian heritage.

Rosemary and Missy exchanged notes about how Roger and I spent too much time playing corporate big shots, leaving them to do the real management job of running a family. Peggy showed off the engagement ring Lee had just given her, well studded with a virtual pyramid of diamonds easily visible from anywhere in the room. By the time the evening ended, everyone seemed to think it had all gone pretty well.

Until the next morning. Even before my first sip of coffee, Alan Pottasch, the advertising director at Pepsi, was on the phone.

"I don't know how to ask this other than directly," he began, "but did Missy order a Diet Coke at the dinner last night?"

"Why, uh, are you, um, asking me that?" I stammered.

Ordinarily, I think I speak fairly fluidly, but this was no ordinary gauntlet he had hurled at my feet. In fact, it was an unthinkable accusation, since both Pepsi and Coke demand total loyalty from their troops in the ongoing battle between them. Drinking the other guy's cola constitutes the closest thing to a capital crime in marketing.

"I'm asking you," replied my client, "because I heard that Roger told someone he was terribly embarrassed in front of Iacocca when Missy ordered a Diet Coke."

Oh, shit, I thought, not just because this ridiculous peccadillo could end up as a career equivalent of driving my Chrysler over a cliff, but also because I knew Missy could well have done it. She doesn't have a politically correct bone in her body. She just doesn't think about things like that, for which she usually has my admiration. But not this time. As I groped for an answer, I decided on a tactic of bravado, however false.

"Look," I said, trying to sound unconcerned while visions of the last mile flashed before me, "I have no idea what Missy ordered. If I would have heard her order a Diet Coke," I continued, "I certainly would have stopped her. I could try to get a copy of the bill to see if it really happened," I suggested, hoping to establish some possibility of a not guilty verdict based on reasonable doubt.

"No, no," Alan replied, "I guess there's nothing you can do about it. Forget it."

For a brief delusory moment, I thought, *Okay, this too shall pass.* Then reality set in.

"Forget it?" I practically gasped. "How can I forget it?

Call me back and tell me Roger's forgotten it, and then I can forget it."

The call ended but the problem didn't. So I called Missy. "Listen," I said, "this may seem like a crazy question but did you order a Diet Coke at the dinner last night?"

"I don't know," she blithely replied, "why do you ask?"

Why indeed? As I said, political correctness has no meaning to this woman. On a political sensitivity spectrum running from zero (completely oblivious) to ten (totally attuned), Missy doesn't even get on the chart. She is the world champion of the politically clueless.

For the next few hours I gave a lot of thought to what else I might do for a living. Or short of that, what penance in addition to the obvious groveling apology might suffice to placate the "terribly embarrassed" head of Pepsi-Cola.

Then Alan called again.

"Hey, guess what?" he jovially intoned. "That whole business about Missy ordering a Diet Coke was nothing. Don't worry about it."

"Are you kidding?" I answered. "Right now my blood pressure could blow the mercury out of the tube, and you tell me not to worry. What happened?"

"It's not important," he said. "It was just a mix-up."

"C'mon," I implored. "You've gotta tell me what's going on. There's a career at stake here."

"Well, it's like this," Alan explained, ignoring the agitation I feigned to hide my relief. "I went and asked Roger if Missy ordered a Diet Coke last night. He says if she did, he wasn't aware of it. I told Roger people were saying that *he said* she did. So he thinks for a minute and then he starts to laugh. He tells me he never actually said that Missy had ordered a Diet Coke. But he says that since he knows Missy pretty well, last night before he left the office for the dinner, he told Rosemary that he *hoped* Missy wouldn't order a Diet Coke and embarrass him with Iacocca. That's all he ever said. Somebody

18

must have overheard him because by this morning, the story went around that he said that's what she *did*. So, no harm done," he concluded, "have a good day."

And I did. In fact, after that, I had a great day.

Joe Louis, the Banker

In dealing with actors, entertainers, and other Hollywood personalities, sooner or later you might have to do business with members of their family — and I don't mean their relatives. The part in *The Godfather* when the Don sends his consigliere to, shall we say, "horse trade" on behalf of a singer who needs a major role in a film in order to save his failing career only thinly veils the actual singer involved. You can be sure the ties were real and binding, not just literary license.

In my case, I got to know the personal manager of one of Hollywood's more prominent names while negotiating a contract for him to star in one of our television campaigns. I had quite a lot of contact with his manager since the commercials proved very successful, running through the year of the agreement plus the second-year option. And I must admit that during all that time, nothing specific about any part of the contract talks or the subsequent production of the advertising suggested Mike Mazzoli was anything other than a legitimate businessman.

(Mike Mazzoli and his associate, Johnny Renatti, are real people. Only their names have been changed to protect the innocent — namely *me*.)

But despite the propriety of our business dealings, I

found it at least curious that Mike alone handled everything with no secretary or other business associates, only a flunky to bring him his espresso, his occasional cocktail, and his ever-present cigars. Not one lawyer or talent agent ever got involved in our discussions. Meetings with Mike took place in the living room of his Beverly Hills house, never in any kind of office. And those sessions invariably began in the late afternoon, with Mike moving deftly around the full-size pool table in his game room, practicing shots as we talked.

Of course, none of that is admissible as evidence of anything. But added to all that, Mike always spoke very softly and dispassionately, in an obviously constricted, high-pitched voice, never raising it in argument, as though suggesting that whatever he said did not require discussion, and certainly not debate. If I seemed unconvinced of whatever point he was making, he very patiently went over it again, never showing a moment's doubt about the outcome of any issue. Mike looked nothing at all like Robert De Niro or Marlon Brando, but if you closed your eyes, you were listening to Vito Corleone.

A few years after this campaign had run its course, I received a very unsettling phone call.

"There's someone named Johnny Renatti on the phone," said my assistant. "He says he's a friend of Mike Mazzoli." I had no idea who Renatti was or what this might be about, but something told me I'd be better off avoiding the call. I realized, however, that if someone in Mike Mazzoli's crowd wanted to talk to me, sooner rather than later, he would.

"Hello," I said, not wanting to offer anything more than necessary.

"Hey, Al, howzit goin'?" Renatti asked rhetorically, not pausing for a response. "Listen, I'm a friend of Mike's," putting an unmistakable emphasis on the word "friend," and adding, "ya know what I mean? Give him a call an' then call me back. Just ask for Johnny."

Discretion overcame valor, preventing me from mentioning that I hate being called "Al," which in fact most people instinctively know not to do. But I suspected Renatti couldn't have cared less. He gave me a number in Las Vegas and hung up. His tone of voice made it clear that he was telling rather than asking me to call Mike. It didn't seem like an instruction I should ignore. I dutifully dialed.

"Mike, it's Allen Rosenshine. I'm calling because—"

"I know," Mike interrupted. "Johnny Renatti called ya."

"Yeah," I replied, "he said I should—"

"I know," he cut me off again. "I tol' him t' call ya. Here's the thing, Allen," he continued. "Do me a favor an' listen t' what he's gonna ask ya. Renatti's got this idea in his head an' I'm tryin' t' help him out. It's somethin' you would know about, so give him a call. Don't worry if ya gotta tell him what he's thinkin' sucks. Just give it to him straight, okay?"

I wasn't at all sure it was okay. "Okay," I replied.

"Hey, thanks, Allen. I appreciate it. By the way," said Mike, "in Vegas they call Renatti 'the viper,' but you don't wanna know why."

I was absolutely sure of that. I called the number Renatti had given me.

"Hello, is, um, er, Johnny there?"

"Hey, dat you, Al? Ya spoke to Mike, right?" He didn't wait for me to answer. "Here's the deal. I'm kinda actin' as business manager for Joe Louis an' I was thinkin' dat he's got jus' as big a name as Joe DiMaggio, so why can't he do TV commercials just like Joe D is doin'? Ya follow me?"

"Yeah, I think so," I replied warily. DiMaggio was a spokesman for a New York bank, pitching it to potential new depositors.

"Good," said Renatti. "What bank do ya think we oughtta go after?"

I didn't like the "we," and I wasn't exactly sure what he meant by "go after," but those were the least of my problems. *How the hell,* I thought, *am I gonna tell somebody called "the viper" that he's out of his insect mind?* You didn't have to be an advertising genius to know that no bank or any financial institution could be represented by an almost inarticulate spokesman who reputedly blew millions of dollars on women and gambling, was accused of tax evasion, and probably couldn't pay even the interest on what he owed.

"You want Joe Louis to advertise for a bank?" I asked rather tentatively, avoiding any suggestion of my immediate reaction.

"You got it, pal. So whaddaya think?"

I thought about Mike's advice that I should tell Renatti the truth. I thought about the possible reasons for Renatti's nickname. I thought about the various parts of my body I preferred to have remain intact. I thought about my wife, my children, and my mother. I ran out of time to think.

"Hey, Al, ya still there?" said Renatti.

"Uh, yeah, Johnny, I'm here."

"So, what bank can ya set Joe up wit?"

I decided to risk everything by following Mike's advice, but not without at least talking to Renatti as deferentially as I would talk to anyone who could materially affect — if not end — my life.

"Y'know, Johnny," I said, "you're absolutely right that Joe Louis is as famous as Joe DiMaggio, so I can understand your thinking. But there's an important difference between the two of them when it comes to being a spokesman for a bank. What I mean is —"

"Hey, I know whatcha saying, Al," he cut in, "but wit fighters, nobody gives a shit if they're colored."

"You're right, Johnny," I said, relieved that he missed the point, giving me something on which I could agree with him again, before telling him why his idea was impossible. But I suddenly had a thought that might convince Renatti not to pursue this, without implying how demented his idea really was.

23

"See, when you use a famous personality like DiMaggio or Joe Louis to pitch for a company," I went on, "you gotta show them how the guy fits their image. DiMaggio is a New York hero, so he's right for a New York bank. Joe Louis is from Detroit, but I don't think any bank in Detroit is big enough to pay what he's worth," I said, eyes closed, praying for a reprieve.

"Joe ain't gonna worry about dat, Al," said Renatti. "Dis guy is so far in hock t' da Feds, he'll do it f' lunch money."

Okay, I thought, *now he's given me a chance, as Mike said, to level with him.*

"That's another problem, Johnny," I said, racing through the opening I saw. "What happens when there are news stories about Joe Louis being bankrupt and not having the money to pay his taxes? I'm not sure how a bank's gonna feel about their guy being broke and a tax delinquent," I finished, as delicately as possible.

The silence could not possibly have lasted as many minutes as it seemed.

"Ah, fuck it," Renatti said finally, "I guess yer right. Tell ya what, Al. I'm gonna think some more an' maybe I'll get back to ya."

His last comment dampened the exhilaration I felt about my diplomatic coup. But I had at least temporarily escaped the sting of the viper.

A few years later, I happened to meet Mike by accident and he asked me if Renatti had ever called again. I told him he hadn't.

"That's good," said Mike. "The guy keeps comin' up wit one crazy idea after another. Y'know what he's tryin' t' push now?"

"No," I replied, "but I can imagine."

"No ya can't," said Mike laughing. "Now he wants t' show people playin' *poker* on TV!"

To this day, I keep wondering. If Renatti *had* called . . .

The Knockout

We were having a tough time on the Gillette Right Guard account. The agency had produced a very famous commercial for Right Guard featuring two men living in an apartment house in which they shared their bathroom medicine cabinet. Discovering his neighbor through the cabinet for the first time, one of the men, a gregarious and funny loudmouth, extolled the virtues of the brand, which they both obviously used. The other, a mousy type, listened in horror and could only respond by plaintively calling his wife.

"*Mona,*" he wailed, delivering the one word by which America came to know, love, and fortunately for us, remember the commercial.

In advertising, the bigger the success, the bigger the potential failure to develop as good a follow-up. We struggled, unable to create an effective sequel. As time and the client's patience wore dangerously thin, we came up with the inspired idea of having the extraverted guy meet his match by opening his medicine cabinet and finding he shared it with a new tenant — none other than boxing's heavyweight champion of the world, Muhammad Ali.

When you use a personality to endorse a product, you have to fulfill two important criteria. First, it must be believable that the celebrity would actually use the product, not a problem in this case. And second, he or she should appear in some context relevant to their fame. Here we took advantage of Ali's penchant for poetry, writing a script in which he could deliver the Right Guard story in rhyme. Everything fell into place. Ali liked the idea, as well as our ode to the deodorant, and agreed to do it. We and the client both believed we had finally outdone the now overdone call for "Mona."

And so we went off to produce the new commercial. We hired a Hollywood director who had experience filming famous people, and who we felt had the kind of personality that would keep someone with the high profile of Ali from overwhelming the shooting. No one really knew anything about Ali personally, and so we were understandably very nervous about how he would behave under the lights of a studio rather than a boxing ring.

We were also not at all sure about Ali's religious or racial sentiments since he had only recently become a Muslim, changing his name from Cassius Clay. Did he view African-Americans and the prejudices against them in the same way as he might have when growing up? Or had his conversion somehow changed his attitudes? Did he consider Caucasians as the oppressors of Muslims just as they had subjugated his race in America since the first slave ship arrived in the New World? Did Muslims have particular sensibilities of which we were ignorant and thus might insult him personally?

We were all on tenterhooks, opting to say little or nothing for fear of saying something wrong.

Our tension was exacerbated by the normal delays, false starts, missed cues, and multiple retakes that ordinarily plague the beginning of any shoot. The anxiety level on the set increased palpably with every one of almost a dozen attempts at the first scene, each of which went wrong for some kind of technical reason. Ali just stood staring straight ahead between each failed take, saying nothing, with none of us daring to say anything to him. Finally, as he waited yet again for the crew to solve whatever problem had spoiled the last shot, he broke both his and our silence.

"Hey, boss," he exclaimed to the director, *"yuh sho' know how t' work a nigger to death!"* And as he started laughing, so did all of us, with obvious relief.

With the mood now far more relaxed, and with some time between finally getting a few good versions of a scene on film and setting up for the next shot, I decided to ask Ali a question that I'm sure occurred to most people aware of the extraordinary amount of money a fighter earns at the championship level.

"Muhammad, I don't mean to put you on the spot like Howard Cosell," I ventured, "but with all the money you and Joe Frazier made from your last fight, how come you haven't scheduled a rematch?"

"Well, first, lemme tell yuh somethin' about me and Cosell," Ali replied. "All that verbal sparrin' we do is just play-actin', y' know, entertainment. We laugh about it all the time. Cosell an' me, we got the best act in sports," said Ali, pausing for a moment.

"Now," he continued, "lemme ask *you* somethin'. Would you drive a car thirty miles an hour into a brick wall for a few million bucks?" Ali asked, not waiting for the answer he knew wouldn't come. " 'Cause lemme tell yuh, man," he went on, "that's what it's like goin' fifteen rounds in a heavyweight fight. Me and Frazier, we don' go partyin' after our fights. We go to the hospital to find out how many ribs we got broken, if our noses or cheekbones or jaws are busted, or our hands got fractured. We get teeth knocked out, our eyes stitched, an' our bodies all bandaged. We wind up with internal bleedin', an' who knows how bad our brains get scrambled? So if you think ah get too much money for what ah do, how 'bout ah give you a million bucks to go one round with me? Or make that one *minute*. You up for it, man?"

"No way, Muhammad," I replied quietly. "Not a chance."

"Didn't think so," he said, smiling, letting me off the hook.

Ali was amazing. He cooperated in every possible way, taking direction and responding like a total professional who acted for a living. He had memorized the poem and never missed a line. When a scene ran a couple of seconds too long and the director tentatively asked Ali if he could shorten his reading by two seconds, the next time he did it exactly two seconds faster. He never complained when he had to just stand on the set doing nothing while the director and his crew fussed with all kinds of adjustments, experimenting with different lighting, various lens settings, sound levels, and camera moves.

Ali did a terrific job for us, and when it was over, he asked us into his dressing room. He clearly had something on his mind that he wanted to talk over with the director. I thought he might have some concern about the commercial, but it had nothing to do with that.

He started by very innocently asking the director, "Hey man, what do yuh do in your life besides shootin' these commercials?"

Our director was not prepared for anything like that, so he hemmed and hawed for a bit before finally answering. "Well, Muhammad," he said, "my real goal is to direct a movie, you know, a feature film."

"What for?" asked Ali. "What good's a movie?"

"Well, a movie can make a statement," said our director, warming to the debate. "It can present a point of view. It can move people to a new level of appreciation and understanding of some important issue," he went on, now feeling the full justification of his objective in life. "A film communicates the human experience and potential. It utilizes all the emotions generated by sight, sound, and motion to create a —"

"Whoa, hey man, cool it," Ali interrupted. "What ah wanna know is, what *difference* does your movie make?"

"I'm not sure I know what you mean, Muhammad," admitted the director.

"It's simple, man," replied Ali. "What ah mean is, what gets changed from the time befo' someone sees your flick to the time after they leave the movie house?"

"Well, I suppose nothing literally changes," the director replied, now somewhat defensively.

"That's it, man," Ali exclaimed. "That's mah point. Your movie's got *no* point, 'cause nothin' changes. Now lemme tell yuh what happens when ah come to town for a fight. Ah leave money in the town. Ah leave a few thousand bucks for the brothers to make a better life. Sometimes ah leave maybe even a few hunnerd thousand to build a club for black kids who ain't got no place to go an' have some good, clean fun. When ah leave town, somethin' is better than it was before ah came. When you finish your movie, everything's just like it was. So what *good* is your film gonna do?"

"Well, if you put it that way, if it's all just a matter of money, I guess I don't know," muttered the director.

"Listen man, whatcha think's gonna change the world 'cept money? Yuh gotta make a lot of it, an' then yuh gotta do somethin' with it. If yuh tell me yuh wanna make movies to make money an' do some good with it, then maybe ah'll even go see wunna your films. Yuh understand what ah'm sayin', mister movie director?"

I think we all did. It was Ali, by a knockout.

Send Out the Clowns

One day, an advertising executive named Phil Joanou, head of an agency in Los Angeles, had an extraordinarily insightful idea. He thought that if advertising skills were being successfully used to sell people products, those same capabilities should be able to "unsell" things people shouldn't buy — specifically illegal drugs. Why can't we use advertising, he reasoned, to deliver anti-drug messages that would persuade and motivate people not to use marijuana, cocaine, heroin, LSD, and other drugs that were ruining people's lives and filling our streets with violent crime?

The answer was startlingly simple. We could.

And as an occupation that doesn't enjoy much respect among the intelligentsia, much less the general public, we should. I hate to admit it, but in survey after survey of the esteem in which various professions are held, advertising invariably ranks right near the bottom, usually below insurance agents, but (with apologies to our Chrysler client) slightly above car salesmen. The opportunity to make an unarguably meaningful and positive contribution to society in a very visible way made Phil's inspiration highly appealing from both a practical, as well as an altruistic, point of view.

Phil took the idea to the American Association of

Advertising Agencies, the trade group whose membership consists of practically all the agencies in the country. He suggested that they should enlist the agencies on a volunteer, pro bono basis to create anti-drug messages for which media companies would then donate time and space for the advertising to be seen. Thus was born the Partnership for a Drug-Free America, a mutual commitment that to this day consists of the agencies that create the advertising and the media that run it.

At the time, the chairman of the 4As, as the association was known, was Lou Hagopian, the head of one of Madison Avenue's larger agencies. To promote Phil's idea, Lou convened a meeting of agency leaders. Having just become chief executive of BBDO, I was among the dozen or so invited.

We met in a conference room in Lou's agency and during the first hour or two developed the premise of having the advertising industry devote its top strategic and creative talent to producing commercials and ads that would "de-normalize" drugs in much the same way that anti-smoking advertising was effectively making lighting up an almost anti-social act. Similar to smoking, illegal drugs, despite their debilitating and often killing effects, had become an almost accepted part of American culture. Through their pervasive presence, they were considered "cool" by a growing percentage of teenagers and young adults.

As we continued to talk through the issues, we were aware that the room was becoming increasingly hot and humid. Realizing that the air-conditioning was not working on this typically muggy July day in New York, we set off to find another room. We had been near Lou's office on the top management floor of his agency, but we were now headed for a conference room in the agency's creative department.

In most agencies, this area bears little resemblance to a business office. Creative people in advertising rarely wear business attire. In fact, they use the word "suits" as a derogatory reference to the account executives and agency managers

31

who represent the clients' views, often in opposition to the ideas the writers and art directors dream up. Jackets, dress shirts, and ties are worn only occasionally when someone from the creative department would attend a meeting with client top management. The more usual attire is mostly T-shirts, chinos or jeans, and sneakers. And beyond the casual dress code, creative departments are generally littered with drawings, photos, old layouts, and such, strewn among funky furniture accessorized by avant-garde artwork and posters.

Through this scene trooped the dozen "suits" representing the leadership of the largest agencies in the business, winding our way through a maze of office chaos. We were on a serious mission in the war on drugs, determined to do something good for America, while possibly even earning some rare plaudits for our industry.

Finally, as we neared the conference room, we heard a voice from one of the cubicles we had just passed. It rose above the cacophony that often accompanies advertising's acts of creation.

"Holy shit," the voice exclaimed in unmistakable distress. "I don't know who those clowns are, but we fucking well better not be getting their account!"

Which perhaps explains two things — first, why I never could take being the head of an advertising agency too seriously and second, why Lou's agency went out of business not too long thereafter.

"Dying Is Easy, Comedy Is Hard"*

Part of an advertising agency's responsibility in producing television commercials for clients is casting the actors and actresses who will play the roles. So agency creative people constantly look to the entertainment world to find new talent who, because they have not yet achieved stardom, will enthusiastically and relatively inexpensively sign on to pitch the clients' products. Thus, one of our creative supervisors introduced a friend, an up-and-coming young comedian, to our creative director, Jim Jordan, suggesting that his friend could play a comic role in one of our commercials.

The creative director in an advertising agency is one of the company's most important managers, and in a large agency such as BBDO, it is always a very demanding job. He or she must decide, many times each day, which ideas for commercials, ads, billboards, and other forms of communication should be shown to clients and recommended for production. Then, if the client approves, the creative director is responsible for insuring that the produced work delivers what has been promised.

*The title of this story is a quote from an eighteenth-century Shakespearian actor, Edmund Kean, reputedly uttered on his deathbed.

A great deal of the client's money rides on these decisions, including the cost of the production and the payment to the media that will show the advertising. Of course, the big question is always whether the advertising will in fact successfully promote the sale of the product. Obviously, if it does, the client and the agency will profit from it. If it doesn't, sooner rather than later, the client will be working with another agency.

The pressures of the job never seemed to get the better of Jim. He took it on with a high level of self-confidence born of considerable ego. He had the uncanny ability to concentrate on the problem at hand, even knowing that many others were percolating and would have to be dealt with almost immediately. Jim could completely focus on the issue in front of him, while totally ignoring a line of people literally outside his office, each waiting to see him with yet another decision to make or problem to solve. Almost always, a conclusion needed to be reached then and there, not put off in a debate of pros and cons. Jim made those decisions, which turned out sometimes right, sometimes wrong, but were never made in doubt. He had a passion for his work and he displayed it aggressively, always with the energy and enthusiasm of a man who enjoyed power, exercised it without equivocation, and rarely if ever looked back at the consequences.

On the day that the aspiring comedian came to the agency to audition, this was the man he faced. Being accustomed to tough audiences, he launched into his performance unfazed by the intensity of Jim's cursory greeting, furrowed brow, and piercing stare. It was a stand-up routine — a calmly delivered, low-key monologue, far more based on wit, subtlety, and sophistication than belly laughs, with no props and no physical action beyond a hand gesture or two and changes in facial expression.

Imagine delivering that style of performance to an audience of one, especially a comedy act you'd expect would generate some level of reaction, from a mild chuckle to a real laugh. But this audition drew only an occasional grunt of acknowledgment from Jim, with not much in the way of even any smiles and clearly no outright laughs. After about five minutes, the comic knew he had laid an egg, but nevertheless politely thanked Jim for his time, and left.

Jim returned to his office and ordered his secretary to get the comedian's friend who had recommended him on the phone.

"That guy's not funny," barked Jim.

"C'mon, Jim, you're kidding, right?" said the comic's friend. "He cracks up everyone who sees his act. He's got star written all over him, and right now we can get him for a song."

"Forget it, he's just *not funny!*" replied Jim, slamming down the receiver for emphasis.

Less than a year later, the comedian's first record album came out. It was called *The Buttoned-Down Mind of Bob Newhart.*

Jim Jordan went on to have a long, well-publicized, and given his penchant for trusting only his own opinions, successful career in advertising. He was surely dedicated to the business, worked incredibly long hours, never seemed to worry about what other people thought of him, and stuck to what he believed with a stubbornness that would make a mule seem compliant. In that sense, you knew what to expect from Jim, and you were almost invariably not disappointed.

You knew what he was. And as it turned out, you knew at least one thing he wasn't. He just wasn't funny.

The Wine Connoisseur

I boarded the 747 jumbo jet fully anticipating the pleasures of traveling first class to Los Angeles, maybe even in the company of a Hollywood personality or two whom I might chat with in the upstairs lounge. It was a time when air travel was still luxurious, before the various managements in that industry drove it — but thankfully not too many of their aircraft — into the ground. And it was long before terrorism forced us to make a flight to anywhere something of a chore.

My early career at BBDO had taken a turn for the better when our client, Gillette, approved a magazine campaign I had written for one of their razors, highlighting its ability to shave a woman's legs without causing nicks and cuts. Naturally, I had suggested we show only the exceptional legs of beautiful actresses and models. Hence to Hollywood and the alluring prospect of casting, about which I had determined not to accept any compromise, but rather to take as long as necessary to find just the right legs attached to just the right women. And I wouldn't have to feel the slightest self-consciousness about staring at as many legs and women as often and for as long as I liked.

And *I'd* be the one to choose who got the job. So as I arrived at the Beverly Hills Hotel, I was feeling very much a part of Hollywood. The only things I lacked were a cigar, a gold necklace, and a pinky ring.

In addition to the pleasure of the company of some of the loveliest, leggiest ladies in the West, I also had the responsibility of hosting the client. I figured that once we had completed shooting the ads that would kick off the campaign, the client might appreciate a dinner with the winners of our little beauty contest. A reservation at a very posh restaurant, in my name of course, awaited us.

The client and I arrived in the obligatory limo, a fashionable thirty minutes late, and only after I had insured that our lovely ladies were already at our table waiting for us. We took our strategically determined seats with budding starlets on either side of us, and began with a champagne toast to the success of our production.

As we looked at the menus, the sommelier presented me with the wine list, which I pretended to study as though I was looking for the particular wine that would best complement the food and properly celebrate the occasion. Actually, since I knew practically nothing about wine, I scanned the names for one that at least I recognized from dinners hosted by others more expert on the subject. Having found a red wine whose name I recalled, I ordered it and was relieved to see the sommelier's ever so subtle nod of approval.

I also remembered having recently read an article about wine that made the point that when you are presented with the cork, rather than sniff it in the popular but apparently irrelevant fashion, you should inspect it for mold, which would indicate a problem with that bottle.

The wine glasses arrived, followed by the sommelier, who carefully opened my chosen bottle and laid the cork to the side of my glass, pouring the traditional small amount for my approval. In my absolute determination to play every moment of this trip to the Hollywood hilt, I ignored the wine so that I could make a point of first checking the cork, not by sniffing it of course, but rather by looking for any telltale sign of mold.

And there it was.

The end of the cork had a distinct black mound of crud on it. *What a stroke of luck,* I thought. *How often do you get to send back a bottle of wine?*

I ceremoniously raised the cork over my shoulder to the sommelier standing behind me, determined that he acknowledge my discovery. As he took the cork from my fingers, I stifled the sense of triumph I felt.

"I believe the cork is moldy," I said quite dispassionately, a comment directed more to the rest of the table than to the sommelier. After only the slightest pause, he slowly returned the cork to the table, laying it carefully next to the hand that a moment before had delivered it with such perfect nonchalance.

I will never forget his words or the barely disguised pity with which he spoke them.

"You are correct, sir," he said. "But we only worry about the end that has been *in* the bottle."

This was one of those moments in life that you can never remember without physically and mentally cringing. The next morning, I again flew first class on the big jet with the lounge, returning from Hollywood, from the Beverly Hills Hotel, and from the bevy of beautiful women whose destinies I had controlled for a little while.

And from then on, if anyone asked me about the Hollywood scene, I could answer with complete honesty that I find it totally embarrasssing.

Slipping on Banana Peels

Chiquita Bananas was one of the first brands I worked on as a copywriter at BBDO. Telling this to anyone has invariably led to a comment like, "Oh, so *you* wrote that jingle," followed by a usually off-key rendition of its most famous line — "Never put ba-na-nas in the re-frig-er-ator." I always explained that the jingle had been written long before my time.

But wanting to explain that whoever wrote it wasn't just being frivolous, I usually added that the reason for that particularly memorable phrase was to encourage people to keep bananas on a kitchen counter or table in plain sight, rather than in the refrigerator, so that they would more likely be eaten sooner. In addition to keeping them out of sight, refrigerating bananas actually makes them last longer, both results that United Fruit, the company that marketed the Chiquita brand, certainly wanted to avoid. To complete this little tutorial on the life of a banana, I should point out that the only negative effect of cold temperatures is that the peel turns black. But the "meat," as it's called, remains perfectly good.

In any event, my job was to write ads about why Chiquita Bananas were better than generic, non-branded bananas, and therefore worth a few cents more per pound. Over the course of a few years, I developed a series of ads, each one telling a particular part of the story of how Chiquita Bananas were specially grown, selectively picked, meticulously inspected, and carefully protected during their shipment from the tropics to the grocery store.

As it turned out, the ads won me a reasonable amount of recognition and quite a few professional awards for creativity, in effect launching my career at BBDO. Because the banana has long been a focal point of jokes, the ads usually had an edge of humor to them. In telling the story of Chiquita's high quality, we always took a light-hearted approach to whatever specific aspect of banana lore we advertised. More often than not, we tried to humanize the fruit, drawing parallels from life to make our points.

For example, to dramatize how Chiquita Bananas were packed for shipping, we showed a banana covered with postage stamps and called it: "The special delivery banana." Or to let people know how the Chiquita growers took extraordinary care of their product, we told the story in an ad headlined: "A man is never so tall as when he stoops to help a banana." To catalog all the research and science that went into trying to grow a better banana, we invented a mythical hybrid fruit that had the peel of a banana but was shaped like a pear, resulting from a hypothetical attempt to cross a banana with an pineapple so as to strengthen its resistance to damage. This tale began with the headline: "A funny thing happened on the way to a better banana." And to offer consumers some of the special knowledge Chiquita people have about bananas, we pictured a banana with various arrows pointing to particular parts of the fruit, accompanied by captions explaining things we thought people would find interesting and helpful in buying it. The headline for this ad was: "How to read a banana."

Eventually, this campaign got me into trouble.

The ad that did it was intended to describe the very demanding criteria that inspectors applied to determine if a banana was good enough to carry the Chiquita label. I titled it:

"What does a banana have to be to be a Chiquita?" The illustration featured a banana with its dimensions written on the skin in the style of a draftsman's drawing, with numbers, inch designations, and arrows along the length and width, showing it to be eight inches long and two-and-a-half inches wide.

But it wasn't an architect or engineer that my ad was using for its prototype. I began the copy by writing: "It's a little like passing the physical to become a Marine." And after more comments about the necessary size specifications a Chiquita Banana had to meet, all done with continuing allusions to the Marines, I ended the ad by saying it all explained why Chiquita was a bigger and better banana, and why, as I wrote: "There aren't many Marines named 'Shorty.'"

It didn't take long for a few advertising critics and quite a few more consumers to accuse United Fruit and BBDO of everything from bad taste to outright pornography. Many of the letters that the client forwarded to me expressed their writers' outrage by offering a graphic suggestion about what I should do with a banana, Chiquita or otherwise.

In the aftermath, what everyone found hard to believe was that I had no intention of making the ad a dirty joke. But I really didn't. (Why would I lie about this, since admitting it makes me look dumb, disingenuous, or both?) Nor would our agency management, much less our client, have approved the ad if they thought it was off-color. We were all just naive, in addition to my being too infatuated with my own cleverness.

But this happened four decades ago. And as we all know, times change. Just think what we could do in today's world with a cigar account.

Assholes with Screwdrivers

Decades before I was born, GE became a BBDO client. And for decades after I came wailing into this world, it remained a very large, very predictable, very dependable, very middle-of-the-road, very uninspiring company, whose advertising very much matched the lack of excitement in its corporate culture.

Until Jack Welch. Soon after Reginald Jones picked Jack as his successor to head GE, the company and its advertising changed dramatically.

Jack came as something of a shock to the GE system, as different in tone of voice and style of management from his predecessor as rap is from opera. Whereas Jones's reputation was pure establishment, refined and reserved, Jack was by comparison a renegade and a revolutionary. Many thought that in the eleventh hour of his otherwise exemplary career, Jones had gone off the deep end by choosing someone so out of the GE character. But in fact, Jones knew what others did not understand — that GE had to change, to modernize, to become more entrepreneurial, more aggressive, and more competitive in its markets. He knew GE needed a leadership injection of youth and energy.

Jones also knew that even though Jack had come up through the GE ranks racking up success after success, at

42

age forty-five, he was a risk. Nonetheless, Jones also knew Jack was the right person for this very big job. His subsequent record at GE left no doubt about the wisdom of Jones's decision.

Jack laid his hands on from day one. He got into everything including the advertising. Not too many chief executives concern themselves with their companies' ads and commercials except to review the advertising occasionally with an eye toward whether they — and sometimes their wives and friends at the country club — liked it. For the chief executive of a company as large, as diverse, and as decentralized as GE to concern himself with scripts, layouts, and unfinished edits of commercials was almost unheard of. But for Jack, advertising became one way for him to show the world GE as he saw it, and as he would revitalize it.

It certainly put the pressure on us as his agency.

Most of it fell on Phil Dusenberry, the brilliantly insightful, classily tasteful, though sometimes insecure creative leader of BBDO in New York. Jack held Phil personally responsible for GE's advertising, although many others helped created it. Phil would have to face Jack across the conference room table, describing in detail every commercial BBDO might suggest to deliver the corporate message of the company. It was Phil who would have to show Jack the final product for his approval before it aired around the world. And Phil would be the one to whom Jack would unhesitatingly direct either his praise or his thankfully less frequent anger when he reviewed the work.

Of the memorable moments of exhilaration or disappointment between GE and BBDO, and between Jack and Phil, one stands out above the others. It took place in the boardroom of the agency, where Phil presented a series of commercials we were recommending we produce for GE. One of these proposed films, entitled "Tinkerers," showed ordinary people innovatively creating quaint solutions to everyday problems with the same entrepreneurial dedication that GE devotes to developing products to meet the needs of their customers. Phil described how the tinkerers' stories would show, for example, a youngster who rigged a series of multiple brushes to simultaneously paint a number of slats on a picket fence. Another vignette would feature a bicycle wheel with paddles made of playing cards stuck in the spokes, driven by the flowing water of a stream to generate electricity for a bulb (GE, of course) to light a tent. Other scenes depicted different types of Rube Goldberg inventions, all dramatizing how people thought up unusual and clever ways to get things done. And as all this played out, an announcer's voice would rapturously celebrate the virtues of these tinkerers, their experiments, and the devices they designed. The tinkerers, in our view, symbolized the inventors and scientists at GE constantly searching for and producing new and better ways to meet the promise of our GE theme, "We bring good things to life." Phil built his presentation to the final moments of the commercial showing Thomas Edison's triumph of illuminating the filament of the first lightbulb as the announcer spoke of GE's heritage and culture having been founded, we had written, "by this greatest tinkerer of them all."

It would be, we all thought, a glorious ode to innovation that Jack could only agree captured the inspirational spirit he sought to infuse throughout GE. As Phil ended his reading of the script, Jack looked directly at Phil through slightly squinted eyes, speaking with a voice struggling to restrain his emotion.

"What are you trying to say, Phil," Jack rasped, "that GE is a bunch of *assholes with screwdrivers*?"

I'd never seen the blood literally drain from a person's face before. Phil looked ashen. His mouth opened slightly, but he didn't say a word.

Jack, apparently oblivious to Phil's distress, went on. "Listen, Phil, at GE, we don't *tinker*," Jack said, almost spitting the word from his mouth with total contempt. "And I don't give a shit about Thomas Edison," he continued. "He's dead, he's history, he's what I want GE to forget." Jack was working himself up to an almost fevered pitch. "Yeah, we're known for lightbulbs and appliances," he said, "but the destiny of GE isn't in the kitchen. Our future belongs to jet engines, diagnostic medicine, space exploration, and new forms of energy. We're not living in the past, and we're not any god-damned *tinkerers!"*

Phil took a few moments to gather his nearly mortally wounded wits. The color returned slowly to his face and he began, a little tentatively but obviously with an idea.

"Okay, Jack," he said, "suppose we kill the word 'tinkerers' and just call the people in the commercial 'pioneers' or 'groundbreakers' or something like that. And then," Phil continued, now gaining confidence as Jack listened, "instead of showing Edison at the end, we could show a rocket blasting off a launching pad or maybe a space station orbiting the earth."

"Yeah, that should do it," Jack airily replied, abruptly ending his diatribe as unexpectedly as he had started it.

And that did do it. That was exactly the commercial he approved and we put on the air a few months later. In the end, it was a piece of cake. But Phil had almost choked on it.

And he wasn't the only one. I must admit, my mouth gets a little dry just thinking about it.

Sonny, That's Acting

I was invited by a client to a charity fund-raising dinner in Washington that was to be attended by President Bill Clinton. About a thousand people had gathered for the event. At the last minute, we were told that the president could not stay very long, but he would join some of us in a small, private reception for just a few minutes before the dinner. Then he had to leave.

As might have been expected, the president was running late, and after the reception had lasted almost an hour behind schedule, he hadn't yet arrived. Realizing that we couldn't wait any longer to start the dinner, we headed for the ballroom and the waiting crowd.

I took that opportunity to use the washroom and was just coming out at the moment President Clinton and his Secret Service detail entered the hotel, heading directly toward me and the ballroom. I stood aside to let them pass and as he approached, I could not help but notice that he looked totally exhausted. He walked slowly with no apparent energy. The man was whipped, beat, dog-tired. As he passed, he glanced at me with a look that said: *I need this like a hole in the head.*

I followed behind the last of his security men as the president entered the ballroom. The band struck up "Hail to the Chief," and the assembled dinner guests burst into applause.

At that moment, the man I had seen in the hallway disappeared.

Almost instantly, in his place stood a tall, beaming, smiling, waving, human dynamo who seemed almost to charge into the room. He moved from person to person, shaking every hand he could reach, stopping for a few words with whomever he recognized. I followed him as he worked his way through the crowd, passing by practically every one of the hundred or so tables. He shook hands, grabbed arms, slapped backs, chatted, laughed, occasionally leaned over to whisper something to someone, and did it all hardly breaking stride.

When he reached the dais, he bounded up to the microphone, thanked everyone for coming, apologized that he couldn't stay, cracked a joke about not missing anything since there was no "Big Mac" on the menu, and headed back out of the room, waving heartily every step of the way.

I had gone back to stand outside the main entrance to see him leave, and just as he came out of the ballroom, he again became the man I had seen going in. His body sagged, his eyes drooped, and he looked drained to the bone. He looked straight at me for a second or two, and with the slightest hint of a smile, just shook his head this time as if to say: *I don't know why I do this.*

But of course, he did.

When I saw President Clinton again at a White House reception a few years later, I wanted to tell him how that evening reminded me of a wonderful joke about acting, but it wasn't the time or the place.

As the story goes, a renowned British director came to New York to stage a Broadway production of *Hamlet,* but he was having great difficulty casting the title role with an American actor. Everyone who auditioned failed to meet his standards, and he had reached the point of canceling the show. However, at the last minute, his agent prevailed upon him to see one more actor who was waiting in the wings to perform.

47

"Very well," he reluctantly agreed, "have him come out."

As the actor emerged from the shadows into the spotlight, the director was appalled.

"What is this, some kind of joke?" he exclaimed, as he watched a stooped over, wizened old man, slowly shuffle across the stage.

"Please don't let him hear you," implored his agent. "He is one of the most famous actors in the Yiddish theater in New York," he continued, "and he begged me to let him read for you. Humor him," he cajoled. "What have you got to lose?"

The director sighed in resignation and called out to the stage, "All right, old chap, let's hear your reading."

The old man peered out at the director through squinting eyes, speaking in broken English with an accent that sounded like he had just come off the boat.

"Listen, misteh, it's okay by you det I doing here deh solilokvee?" he asked.

The director rolled his eyes, thinking, *Am I to be spared nothing?* "Yes, my dear fellow, whatever you like, but do get on with it," he answered.

With that, the old man began to stand up straight, squaring his shoulders in a commanding posture, raising his head to reveal a look of pure determination, with eyes that no longer watered but were fixed on the director with a piercing stare. He then proceeded to deliver Hamlet's soliloquy with perfect Shakespearean diction in the most inspired interpretation the director had ever heard. Finally, as he uttered the last words of his reading, the actor slowly collapsed into the small, hobbled figure he had been, once again straining to see through narrowed eyes.

"Vas det vat you vas looking for, misteh?" he asked.

"Good God, man, that was absolutely brilliant," replied the director, recovering from his mesmerized silence. "Larry never did it better. But how is it possible," he asked, "for someone like you to totally transform yourself into the very essence of Hamlet?"

The old man slowly smiled at the director. "Sonny, det's eckting!" he replied.

But he wasn't acting. For those few minutes, he *was* Hamlet. And for that half hour back in that ballroom, Bill Clinton was Bill Clinton.

A Tie for Christmas

Back in the days when BBDO still had a Madison Avenue address (almost no agencies actually remain there today), the company's top executives all had offices in one area of one floor. Perhaps this explains the insular nature of that group, although with the exception of them all being white male Christians, their personalities varied considerably. Walter Wakefield (in his case, an alias) certainly differed greatly from the others.

Whereas most of them had enlarged egos along with the highly developed shrewdness usually necessary to succeed in the ad business, Wally was a self-effacing, straight shooter — a truly decent guy who literally lived by the Boy Scout Law. He was trustworthy, loyal, helpful, friendly, courteous, kind, obedient, cheerful, thrifty, brave, clean, and reverent — everything the mantra demanded.

His cohorts left the long hours and drudgery of the business to those on the floors below them. Wally arrived in his office before sunrise, hours before anyone else, pacing back and forth as he dictated long and detailed memos into his tape recorder, summarizing every phone call or meeting of the previous day to initiate whatever anally compulsive follow-up he always believed necessary. And as most of his colleagues assembled promptly at five o'clock every afternoon in the chairman's office for a round or ten of drinks, Wally labored on at his desk, rarely allowing liquor to impair his acute sense of responsibility.

While most members of this executive suite were pretty savvy in the ways of business and corporate politics, Wally's overwhelming naiveté made him a marked man among the boys who found practical jokes irresistible.

Wally's first Christmas on the executive floor provided a perfect opportunity to test the limits of his trusting nature. A few mornings before the holiday, one of the executive vice presidents, in cahoots with the others, ambled into Wally's office, casually asking a question regarding the agency's chairman, Charlie Brower.

"Say, Wally boy," the designated instigator asked, "did you get Charlie his tie for Christmas?"

"What d' you mean?" Wally asked.

"Don't you know that Charlie loves wacky ties? He's been collecting them for years. The crazier the better. Most of us give him one every Christmas. The ties always get a big laugh out of him."

"Okay, thanks for the tip," said Wally.

That afternoon, he walked over to Times Square, and from the tackiest souvenir shop he could find, he bought an amazingly garish tie sporting a hula dancer whose hips appeared to sway when the tie moved. Then on Christmas Eve, Wally dutifully walked into Charlie's office to wish him a happy holiday.

"Merry Christmas, Charlie," said Wally, handing him the gift.

"Thanks, Wally," said Charlie, inspecting the box. "It looks like a tie."

"Yeah," Wally eagerly replied. "I think you'll like it."

"Okay, mind if I open it?"

"No, go right ahead," said Wally.

He stood patiently in front of Charlie's desk as he tore off the wrapping. Charlie opened the box and for a few seconds stared at the hula dancer, who stood motionless, not undulating at the moment.

"She moves whenever you move the tie," said Wally.

"Are you out of your god-damned mind, Wakefield?" said Charlie, who never met a word he thought he should mince. "What made you think I'd wear a piece of shit like this?" The dancer danced as Charlie waved the tie in front of Wally's face.

Wally, taken momentarily by surprise, replied, "I know you don't really wear these ties, Charlie. It's for your *collection*."

"What do you mean 'these ties'? What ties? What 'collection'? What the fuck are you talking about?"

Surprise had turned to stunned shock. Wally thought he might faint, but he only fell silent. A few seconds later, and well before Wally, Charlie put it together. "Wakefield," he sighed, "sometimes you're a real jerk. Get the hell out of here."

Thus, the Christmas tie with the hula dancer took its place in BBDO history.

I liked working with Wally because you always knew that what you saw was what you got. You would have thought having done a stint in counter-intelligence before joining BBDO, he might have learned to fake left and go right at least occasionally. But he was just too honest for his own good.

The following year, no one figured to pull the same stunt on Wally again. Surely even he would be wise to it. And indeed, he had his guard up as the holiday approached. This was Charlie's last Christmas before retiring, and Wally had determined not to repeat his previous gaff. He would send Charlie off with a meaningfully appropriate gift. Not trusting any advice he might get from the surrounding offices, he decided to ask Charlie's wife what he might really like. So he phoned her.

"Mrs. Brower, this is Walter Wakefield at the agency. I'd

like to ask you what I could get Charlie for Christmas before he retires."

"Why Walter," she replied, "that's really sweet of you." She paused for a moment before saying, "You know, Charlie has always wanted to learn how to cook, so he plans to take a course now that he'll have the time. Why don't you get him something he could use for his cooking lessons?"

"Great," said Wally, thanking her profusely.

And off he went to buy a beautiful set of copper pans, which he proudly presented to Charlie on the day before Christmas. As he opened the gift, Charlie looked warily at Wally.

"Well, it's much too big for another tie," said Charlie, somewhat uncharitably.

"Nope," said Wally, enthusiastically brimming with confidence. "This is something I know you'll really like."

Opening the box, Charlie looked inside, looked at Wally, looked in the box again, looked at Wally again, and finally spoke with quiet resignation.

"Wally," he said, "what the hell do you think I'm gonna do with a bunch of fucking frying pans?"

This time, Wally just bowed his head in frustration as he realized the lengths to which his prankster buddies had gone. This time, they had enlisted Charlie's wife in their plot to make a fool of him with the chairman, once again.

But this time, Wally got from Charlie what he had been promised the year before. He got that big laugh, to which Charlie added a heartfelt "Merry Christmas."

The Affliction

After having created a very successful commercial starring Muhammad Ali for Gillette Right Guard, we were hard pressed to come up with something new that could generate equal notoriety and impact. Ali's star power had helped boost Right Guard's sales and we needed a way to continue the trend. Using another famous personality seemed the obvious solution, but it had to be someone whom we could relate to the product in some relevant way. Just having well-known names say they use a product is not an effective way to capitalize on them.

In addition, a deodorant is not the kind of product most celebrities would want to endorse. It makes sense for an athlete, but what leading man or woman would want to talk publicly about a product he or she uses to prevent underarm sweat and odor?

The problem was solved when one of our creative people thought of Don Rickles. We had often used humor in Right Guard advertising because the nature of the category could lead to funny situations. So a famous comedian was a natural choice. But even that connection wasn't enough. There had to be a specific and credible reason why a particular comic would care about the product, which is why the idea of using Rickles was an inspiration.

His humor had always been based on insulting people, making fun of them, or in our terms, "making them sweat." Our logic was that Right Guard would therefore be a product he would hate, a product he would not want people to use, a product he would tell people *not* to buy since it worked against his interest. And beyond the product itself, the people who made it — our client, Gillette — would become the natural object of his scorn.

This idea led us to create some very funny commercials, tailored to Rickles's act, making use of his attack-dog delivery, his phraseology, and his unique ability to subject the objects of his mock disaffection to an onslaught of utter distain. In one spot, he would regale a mythical president of Right Guard with epithets ranging from "hockey puck," a typical Rickles insult, to calling him "the underarm biggie." In another, he would warn him to stop marketing Right Guard. "You keep selling this stuff," Rickles would say, "and *you'll* be paying for my mother's apartment in Miami Beach." In still another assault, he would threaten to find out where the Gillette executive lived, and "drown his rubber duck." And all the while, Rickles would complain bitterly about how effectively Right Guard works, which was our rationale for why he was so angry about it, and exactly what we wanted the consumer to hear.

In accordance with their established procedures and because it was highly unusual to promote a brand by having a famous personality insult it, Gillette tested our Rickles concept with consumers before agreeing to produce it. It achieved the highest scores they had ever seen for memorability and delivery of the product message.

When it came time to actually produce the commercials, everyone was on edge as to how Rickles would behave during the filming. Would he be cooperative or would he resent taking orders from a guy who directs commercials rather than television shows or Hollywood films? Would he follow the script and deliver an advertising copywriter's lines or would he insist on ad libbing as he always did in his act? Would he maintain his comedic energy over the many times scenes had to be shot and reshot to insure that we would have the footage we needed to edit the commercial exactly as we had promised the client?

We were nervous, the director was nervous, the client was nervous, and apparently, as the first scene of the first commercial was being taped, so was Rickles. Because as the camera rolled and he began to speak, a line of spittle started running out of the corner of his mouth. The more worked up he became in accosting the Right Guard product and the people who made it, the more saliva ran from this mouth and down his chin, clearly caught in the glare of the intense camera lights and obvious for all of us to see.

"Oh my God," I heard the client exclaim under his breath, "do you see that? What the hell is *that*?"

"I don't know," was the extent of the explanation I could muster.

"What are we gonna do?" the client hissed through a jaw now clenched in panic.

"I don't know," I whispered back, in what was becoming a refrain.

"Has that ever happened to him before?" he asked plaintively.

"I don't know," I muttered predictably.

At that point, the director yelled, "Cut!"

Rickles jumped from the stool he'd been sitting on to deliver his monologue, pulled a handkerchief from his pocket, and rushed over to me while wiping the wad of spit that had gathered prominently on his chin.

"That was great!" Rickles exulted. "I'm telling you, Allen," he exclaimed, "not even I could do it any better than that. You don't even need another take. Let's go. I'm ready for the next scene," he said, turning back to the set.

The client had gone pale as a ghost. I wasn't feeling too good either.

"Wait a minute," he gasped. "Is he serious? What about that *stuff* running down his chin?"

"Hey, what are you, a wise guy?" Rickles yelled, turning back to face us. "Are you makin' fun of me?" he said, looking right in the client's face. "Lemme tell ya somethin' about that 'stuff runnin' down my chin,' " he snarled in a perfect imitation of the client's bleating tone. "Sometimes it happens, ya know what I mean? An' then I can't do anythin' about it. An' if ya don't like it, that's too bad, 'cause we both gotta live with it. It's an affliction."

With that, Rickles wheeled around and stalked back to his stool. But not before he glanced at me and winked.

Finally realizing that this had all been an elaborate joke, I breathed a sigh of relief. My client, who hadn't seen Rickles wink, and whose knees were practically buckling, sank slowly into his seat and just sat there holding his head in his hands.

"Hey, Allen, spray him with the Right Guard," Rickles shouted. "I think he's having an underarm attack."

"That's not funny, Don," I said trying to restore at least a semblance of my client's dignity.

"Yeah, it is," Rickles shot back. "It's fuckin' hysterical!"

And he was right. Every time I see Don Rickles, I still laugh about it. The client? Probably not, even though his advertising was a huge success.

Wo Ist de Herrenzimmer?

During the early '70s, when BBDO first began to build its network of companies outside the United States, I had numerous occasions to meet people from other countries, primarily in Europe. Our objective was to find agencies in the major international markets with which we could establish working relationships, including ownership positions, by purchasing a percentage of their equity. We looked for agencies whose work we liked, whose cultures we could share, and whose managers we believed would be good people with whom to do business.

Of course, the process worked both ways. We needed to convince prospective partners that we offered them the same qualities. More than just financial compensation for their equity, they were looking for professional advantages we might bring to their businesses. So when the various courtship visits were exchanged, we went out of our way to demonstrate how our experience, knowledge, methodologies, and professional talent could enhance the other company's opportunities.

One of BBDO's acknowledged strengths during those years was our research capabilities. We put a great deal of investment and energy into developing research protocols that would enable us to understand what consumers wanted from the products and services our clients offered, and how best to align our clients' brands with consumer desires. We often had methods for successfully developing advertising strategies that many of the European agencies we were negotiating with did not. Research thus became an important selling point in our efforts to convince these agencies that we could help them become more competitively successful in their respective countries.

If any part of advertising can be considered a science, research would surely qualify. Whereas the creative product — the television and radio commercials, the magazine and newspaper ads, the posters and billboards, and many forms of more contemporary messages driven by new communications technologies — is always exposed to personal opinion and evaluation, consumer research produces far more quantitative and objective measurements.

Our director of research during the years we began to form our international network was a well-educated and intelligent proponent of research, and an innovator of various proprietary BBDO procedures. He held a doctorate in psychology, and his staff included people with advanced degrees in a variety of subjects related to the research mission. When we met with foreign agency principals to whom we were anxious to offer tangible benefits for joining our network, our research programs and the man who led them became prominent features in our presentations and discussions.

One of the most important countries in which we needed to establish a partnership was Germany. So I and fellow emissaries from BBDO, including our research director, traveled to Düsseldorf to meet with the management of a leading agency with whom we were anxious to come to terms. During the course of the visit, our hosts took us for dinner to the Altstadt, the older section of the city, where we ate at a centuries-old inn that maintained much of the decor and style of far earlier times.

The menu featured recipes handed down through many

generations. In particular, we were offered a pepper pot soup that came with a warning it might be the spiciest dish any of us had ever tasted. Our hosts joked about it in a way that could be taken as a challenge to our willingness to risk inflaming not just our mouths, but also deeper parts of our digestive tracts.

Our research director saw their comments as a culinary contest of some sort. "I love spicy foods, the hotter the better," he declared with great bravado. "I'll try it!"

In this case, I did better research than he. I decided not to have the soup, having noticed that not one of our local colleagues had ordered it. When the dish was delivered, our researcher dove right in under the watchful and already smiling eyes of the Germans.

"This is delicious," he declared triumphantly, continuing with another few spoonfuls.

As many of us have experienced, sometimes it takes a few moments for really spicy foods to register on our palates, possibly because they are momentarily numbed by the shock of the fiery assault on our taste buds. After a few more seconds, our research director slowly put down his spoon, bowed his head, and sat absolutely still.

I watched in amazement as first his forehead, then his face, then his neck literally turned red. Sweat broke out almost instantaneously across his entire brow.

Our hosts began to laugh heartily at his distress, not at all surprised, but nonetheless finding it quite funny. It was clear to me, however, that the guy was really suffering and was paying a steep price for his jaunty foray into local custom. He then signaled to a passing waiter, and wanting to demonstrate to our hosts that he could still deal with the situation without showing any further cultural lack of awareness, he decided to speak in German.

"*Wo ist de herrenzimmer?*" he managed to croak through his pain. He had assumed that "men's room" was translated literally as a combination of *herren,* which means "men," and *zimmer,* meaning "room."

The waiter burst out laughing while the chortling of our hosts grew even more intense. He replied in English, making it absolutely clear he knew he had not been addressed by a German.

"Ze *herrenzimmer* iss in ze kessel up ze hill," he said, pointing upward and outward from the restaurant, provoking even more laughter. In fact, the *herrenzimmer* was indeed in a castle on a hill outside the city. The word actually means a room from antiquity in which men would smoke and drink after dinner, having taken leave of their ladies.

Happily, the story ends with our research director finding his way to the men's room, dousing his face and neck with cold water, returning to the table quite chastened and very humble in accepting that he had been the butt of a typically unsubtle German joke, which he had compounded by his own ignorance.

Maybe it helped that our hosts could make some fun of the people who were, in effect, trying to buy their agency. Which, in the end, we did.

Star Chatting

When I became president of the the BBDO headquarters agency in New York, Phil Dusenberry succeeded me as creative director. During the more than twenty years that he oversaw the agency's broadcast and print advertising on behalf of many of America's most iconic brands, he became a legendary figure in the advertising community, responsible for a large body of truly memorable, inspirational, and on many occasions, award-winning work.

One of Phil's most often stated beliefs about advertising is that it should be famous. Certainly, the more people recognize a campaign, and the more it gets talked or written about, the more effectively it promotes the brand it represents. And to accomplish this, Phil believed that whenever appropriate to the product, not to mention affordable to the client, advertising should make use of highly visible personalities, especially the biggest stars in entertainment and sports.

Of course, Phil understood that you don't use just any big name for just any brand. He always saw to it that there was a clear and relevant reason why a particular famous person would be in a commercial for the specific brand being advertised. It would strain credulity, for example, to see Britney Spears shopping in a Wal-Mart. Somehow, her concern for their "always low prices" would not ring true. But Britney singing and dancing for Pepsi is another and far better story.

In any event, Phil was a vocal proponent and constant practitioner of using famous people so that their renown might rub off on our clients' brands. One day, on a flight to Los Angeles to produce a television campaign, he thought he might pull off one of the great coups in the history of the business by enlisting an actor of unparalleled stature.

He had settled into his first-class seat and as the time for take-off approached, it seemed as though the seat next to him would remain unoccupied. As more minutes passed and no one showed up to sit with him, Phil became convinced that he'd have that extra seat to spread out his belongings.

Then, as the flight attendant began the seat belt demonstration, there was a small commotion as other attendants rushed through the aisles, and a rising murmur came from the passengers around him. Just as he turned his head to see what was happening, a very large man literally plopped himself into the empty seat with an audible exhalation of breath and began wiping the sweat from his brow. When the man finally took his handkerchief away from his face and reached to put it back in his pocket, Phil knew immediately that he was about to spend the next six hours sitting next to Marlon Brando.

Wow, Phil thought, *what an opportunity!* His mind began racing with the possibilities. *Imagine being the first agency to use Marlon Brando in a commercial.*

From considerable experience, Phil knew that under ordinary circumstances, this would be an extremely difficult thing to accomplish. You'd have to go through agents, managers, lawyers, and an entire obstacle course of ego and greed before you'd get anywhere near a star of Brando's magnitude. But there Phil sat, shoulder to shoulder with the man himself, a mere inches away with nowhere to go except sit there.

What a home run this could be, Phil exulted. *No, not just a home run. A grand slam! I've got hours to pitch him person-*

ally on the idea. No flunkies to get in the way. Just me and Marlon.

But wait a minute, Phil brought himself up short. *What am I pitching him about? Could he do a Pepsi spot? Nah,* he thought, glancing furtively at Brando's considerable girth, *it'd have to be* Diet *Pepsi and their budget isn't big enough. Would he appear as the Godfather? No way,* Phil figured, *we'd have to pay Coppola a fortune. Well, maybe I don't have to make it that specific. Maybe I can just get him interested in the idea of doing a commercial, and we can kick it around for a while. Yeah, that's it,* Phil concluded, *I can explain to him how the right commercial could enhance even his image, maybe by doing something really funny or playing a role he hasn't tried before. Whatever, but I gotta talk to him.*

Just as Phil was about to break the ice, the attendant stopped at their seats and asked Phil what he'd like to drink. "Just a club soda," said Phil, who rarely drinks and was certainly determined to keep a clear head to capitalize on this fortuitous opportunity.

"Champagne," said Brando, reclining his seat and closing his eyes.

Damn it, thought Phil, *I gotta get to him before he falls asleep. But his eyes are shut. I can't talk to him when his eyes are shut. I'll have to wait till they bring the drinks.*

A few minutes later when the drinks arrived, Brando opened his eyes as though on cue, just as his champagne was being set on the armrest between him and Phil. As he reached for the glass, his body shifted and turned slightly toward Phil, who saw this as his cue.

"Excuse me," said Phil, "but I couldn't help noticing —"

Without so much as looking at Phil, Brando cut him off with a hand raised in regal disdain, palm extended almost in Phil's face.

"Please," said Brando with a heavy sigh and an expression that bespoke the weariness of a man for whom people are a constant intrusion, "no conversation."

And not another word passed between them for the next six hours, every second of which must have been an eternity to Phil.

But Phil is nothing if not stubborn in the pursuit of a good advertising idea. Some years later, we had another chance to enlist Brando, this time successfully, when he performed as the voice of a little girl talking like Vito Corleone in a commercial we did for Pepsi.

And that time, Phil and Brando had a very good conversation.

Which is more than can be said about three other megastar sightings — one involving Charlie Miesmer, a long-time creative lieutenant of Phil's, another including me, and the last with Jim Jordan, for whom all of us worked at one time.

Like Phil's encounter, Charlie's took place on a plane where he found himself seated next to Willie Mays some years after he had retired from baseball. Charlie, a wonderful advertising creator rarely stumped by the written word, suffers from a slight stutter, which becomes more obvious when he gets excited, certainly the case with Mays sitting right next to him. But he was determined to say something to the legendary ball player. As the plane taxied out to the runway for takeoff, Charlie finally worked himself up to the occasion.

"Eh-eh-excuse me, but I juh-just gotta tell you that you've been my huh-huh-hero ever since I was a kid. But don't wuh-worry. I won't be annoying you all th-th-through this trip," said Charlie, putting out his hand, and smiling with relief.

Mays said nothing in reply. He looked at Charlie, grimaced slightly, unbuckled his seatbelt, and moved a couple of rows away.

My moment came with Christopher Plummer when we

were both on a dais at a dinner honoring a mutual acquaintance. I had just recently seen him on Broadway in *Barrymore*. He had given a brilliant performance — one great actor playing another. As we took our seats at the head table, I took the opportunity and congratulated Plummer on his truly remarkable talent.

"Yes, I know," he replied, turning away.

I remained staring at his back, wishing I had been quick enough to compare his John Barrymore to Captain von Trapp, the nauseating role he played in *The Sound of Music*. Or better yet, to offer my condolences on his failure to beat out Jason Robards, Jr., when they had both auditioned as announcers for one of our Pizza Hut campaigns.

But if Charlie and I were once undone by events of unrequited hero worship, Jim Jordan was eviscerated.

He had escorted a beautiful young woman to a cocktail party where he was thrilled to find that one of the guests was his baseball idol, Joe DiMaggio. Not at all bashful, Jim introduced himself to DiMaggio, proudly presenting his date as well. He then proceeded to regale DiMaggio with his many memories of Joltin' Joe's home runs, his great catches playing centerfield in Yankee Stadium, and his famous, record-setting, fifty-six-game hitting streak.

Shortly after DiMaggio left the party, one of the waiters informed Jim's date that she had a phone call. She returned, looking somewhat distracted.

"What's the problem?" Jim asked.

"That was Joe DiMaggio on the phone," she replied. "He wanted to know if I could ditch the creep I'm with and meet him later."

Nice guys, these immortals be.

The Stanhope Code

I first met Keith Reinhard, head of the Needham Harper advertising agency, in the mid-'80s, a time when agencies, among many other kinds of companies, were in the throes of the merger mania that gripped American business for the better part of the last two decades of the twentieth century. Fueled by undiscriminating investors pouring money into junk bonds, and egged on by investment bankers and lawyers collecting huge fees for raising capital and structuring corporate consolidations, companies were in a frenzy of buying each other, merging with each other, and in many cases destroying each other in the process.

In the advertising industry, the buyer with the bucks, driven by unlimited ego and an insatiable appetite to become the biggest in the business, was a company called Saatchi & Saatchi. It was named for the two British brothers who founded it, Charles and Maurice, who were devouring everything in sight for prices most everyone except the Saatchis thought were absurdly overblown. With the brothers on an acquisition rampage, Keith and I shared the same concern — either or both of our companies could conceivably become takeover targets to help fulfill the Saatchis's dream of an advertising empire.

Coincidentally, Keith and I had moved along almost parallel career paths. We had both come up through the ranks of our agencies as writers, eventually moving into general management. We're within a few years of each other in age. And we had both become heads of our respective companies at about the same time, which *New York* magazine had chronicled in an article featuring the two of us together, even though we had never met.

Our professional similarities far outweighed the cultural differences between us — Keith, a slow-talking, Midwestern Episcopalian, and I, a New York Jew who could talk fast enough to recite the complete Declaration of Independence while Keith would not yet have gotten to pursuing happiness. Some years after we met, while trading tales about our early years in the business, Keith told me that the most exciting thing that had happened to him during his first advertising job was a phone call from home in Indiana telling him that the wind had blown the roof off the henhouse. He's come a long way since then. Not even a force-five hurricane could blow anything off any of the homes he owns today.

I called him and suggested we get together. In the milieu of everybody talking to each other, and the Saatchis talking to most of us, he suggested that we find a place not frequented by our colleagues or competitors. That way, our meeting would not result in public speculation that could unsettle clients or staffs enough to make a deal difficult, if not impossible, to pursue. Since we both lived on Manhattan's upper east side, we decided on an early breakfast at the Stanhope, a small hotel in our neighborhood.

We met, we talked, and we agreed on practically everything important to a potential merger that could strengthen our respective operations and fend off the brothers Saatchi. We quickly found that we shared the same view of an advertising agency's role in serving clients. We had the same priorities as to how success should be measured in our business. We had similar opinions about the state of the business and the nature of our respective agencies' vulnerability to the onslaught of the Saatchis. And most important, we honestly felt that a potential combination of our companies could provide truly complementary strengths under the umbrella of a shared culture. This, despite the fact that everyone talking up a merger always predicts big benefits from all kinds of synergies that in fact almost never materialize.

When we had finished our conversation and decided to meet again, Keith had another suggestion about keeping our discussions out of the rumor mill or worse yet, the press, a very difficult thing to do in a business where the life expectancy of a secret is measured in minutes.

"Whenever I work on anything confidential," Keith said in his typically halting manner, "I give it a code name. I'm calling this one 'Project Stanhope' and," he continued after his usual pause, "if we have to phone each other, we can just use that instead of our names."

"Okay," I replied. "Nice to meet you, Mr. Stanhope."

"Likewise, Mr. Stanhope," said Keith. We shook hands and left the hotel, separately of course.

I had barely sat down at my desk before my assistant buzzed me. "Keith Reinhard is calling," she announced.

"Who?" I blurted out, followed by a quick "Never mind," not wanting her to repeat his name. "I wonder why he's calling," I made a point of saying as I picked up the phone.

"What are you doing, Keith?" I asked with some alarm. I thought we agreed to keep a lid on this. What happened to 'Mr. Stanhope'?"

"Well, Allen, I don't think that's going to work," said Keith slowly.

"Why not? What's the problem?" I shot back, as impatient as he was unrushed.

"Well, here's what happened," said Keith, "See, I have, a regular routine for my assistant to let my management group know where I'll be during the day so they can reach me at any time."

"Yeah, so?" I urged him on.

"Well this morning, she sent around my schedule and the first thing on it was, well here, let me read it to you," said Keith. "It says 'Project Stanhope meeting with Allen Rosenshine.' So that means at least half a dozen people here already know about our meeting."

"And by now," I replied, "that half dozen have told another dozen, and they in turn have no doubt told at least two dozen here at BBDO."

"Yep," said Keith, this time without a moment's hesitation.

So that morning saw the first and last meeting of Project Stanhope, followed by a flurry of denials at our respective agencies that anything was going on between us. And I didn't see Keith again until some time later when we began new talks about bringing our agencies together in a different deal with, of course, a different code name.

This time, we were talking about the creation of what would become the Omnicom Group, which in addition to our two agencies would also include Doyle Dane Bernbach — a unique merger of three agencies under one new holding company. The code name for these meetings was "4801," derived from the suite number in the Helmsley Palace Hotel where all our joint planning took place. Surprisingly, we were able to keep this a secret for practically all of the nine weeks it took to put the merger together, the only leaks coming in the final week when trade press reporters were camped outside our agencies to see who might be going in and out. We even had a bomb threat during a BBDO board meeting, intended to see if anyone from another agency might exit the building along with us in the ensuing evacuation.

But the Stanhope code had taught Keith and me our lesson. The press never caught on. And the only bomb that went off was the front-page story in the *New York Times* when we announced the Omnicom deal, which caught the advertising world by complete surprise.

Hai, Hai, Henry

A few months after the 9/11 terrorist attack on New York, Mayor Rudy Giuliani asked our agency to develop a television campaign to promote tourism, which had diminished precipitously after the destruction of the World Trade Center towers. Giuliani believed that commercials celebrating the spirit of the city would not only send a message of optimism to potential visitors, but also encourage New Yorkers as they tried to cope with the new realities of the losses already incurred, along with the prospect of living under continuing threat.

The concept BBDO created for this campaign was to highlight the uniqueness of the city and its people by dramatizing what we called "The New York Miracle." The idea was that New Yorkers are people with dreams about their lives that the special qualities of the city make possible. The commercials would show people living their dreams, and invite others to visit the city and share that feeling.

We thought that to make these commercials highly impactful and memorable, the people who appeared in them should be New Yorkers who were well known the world over. We knew that we could enlist many highly recognizable personalities who would, like us, be willing to donate their efforts to the cause of supporting their city during this difficult time.

And the spokesperson inviting tourists to visit would be Giuliani himself. Putting clients in their commercials is usually a rather cynical ploy to insure that they will like what they see. But in this instance, Giuliani spoke for New York as no one else could.

Beyond the emotional appeal of the " miracle" notion and the big names who would portray it, we also felt that we should not be overly serious or run the risk of appearing maudlin at a time when people needed cheering up. We determined that the dreams our stars would depict for themselves would actually make a little fun of them, of who they were, and what they had already achieved in their successful careers. We speculated correctly that under the circumstances, they would willingly go along with some self-deprecating humor.

And so they did.

Woody Allen appeared on the Rockefeller Center ice rink, doing spins, leaps, and acrobatics worthy of a professional skater (who was, in fact, his "double"). He then claimed this was the first time he had ever been on skates. Barbara Walters came out on a Broadway stage to audition for a musical, singing her number horrendously off-tempo and out of tune, a perfect parody of someone with a totally tin ear. The tux-and-tails-clad conductor of a concert performed by the New York Philharmonic turned out to be Yogi Berra. Robert De Niro and Billy Crystal, one dressed as a Pilgrim and the other as a turkey for Macy's Thanksgiving Day parade, argued hilariously over who should play the turkey. A heavyset, older man in a business suit walked to home plate in an empty Yankee Stadium, pointed like Babe Ruth toward the bleachers, pretended to swing at an imaginary ball, and lumbered around the bases, ending with a head-first slide across home plate. As he rose from the dirt, dusting himself off, we saw it was Henry Kissinger, an avowed baseball fan, acting out his dream.

The campaign achieved instant notoriety. It was picked up by the news media and publicized not only in the U.S., but literally all around the world, including one country where we had only recently been doing business — Japan.

We had been the first company to acquire a Japanese advertising agency as part of a global network. In addition to being a historically insular culture, the Japanese are also a very polite and reserved people not given to displays of emotion, especially in meetings with foreigners. We had to work quite hard at earning their trust before they would become actively involved with us as business partners. This required us to visit them, meet their clients, their top media executives, and on one occasion in early 2002, to pay a courtesy call on an important Japanese politician, Tamisuke Watanuki. In the Japanese central government, Mr. Watanuki was the equivalent of our Speaker of the House.

When we arrived at Mr. Watanuki's living quarters, part of a complex of government buildings situated amid beautiful and perfectly manicured gardens, we were ushered into a very formal meeting room, simply but elegantly furnished with an abundance of highly polished wood, everything immaculately pristine. A few minutes later, Mr. Watanuki entered the room, an elderly man as most Japanese business and political leaders tend to be, impeccably groomed and dressed in a perfectly tailored suit.

As head of BBDO, I was introduced to him through our respective translators, and after the traditional bows and exchanges of business cards, we sat to begin the meeting. The chief executive of our Japanese agency explained who we were and the nature of the new business relationship between our companies. Mr. Watanuki listened with polite attention but apparently little interest, sitting rigidly without moving a muscle or changing his dispassionate expression.

Finally, when it was time for him to respond, he expressed his sympathy for the attack on New York, and asked if the city had begun the process of renewal. Despite the obvious fact that this was not to be an advertising discussion, I cited the work

BBDO had done with Mayor Giuliani on "The New York Miracle" advertising. I mentioned to Mr. Watanuki that he knew one of the people who appeared in our commercials, having been briefed by my Japanese colleagues that he had been in numerous meetings with Kissinger. To my astonishment, and judging from their faces, to the equal shock of Mr. Watanuki's entourage, when he heard Kissinger's name, he leaped from his chair, threw his arms over his head and jumped toward me in the way Kissinger had started his slide into home plate in the commercial. To this, Mr. Watanuki added what sounded like a Samurai war cry, shouting, *"Hai, hai,* Henry!"

His translator, as stunned as the rest of us, recovered enough to stammer, "He, uh, um, he says, 'yes, yes, Henry.' "

Mr. Watanuki went on to tell us, with much excitement and many animated gestures, how much he liked our advertising, which in fact had never run in Japan, but had been shown on many Japanese news programs.

That commercial and that meeting with Mr. Watanuki went a long way toward convincing our Japanese colleagues that we were the right people to help guide their eventual assimilation into a Western business association. And it assured me that in any culture, regardless of its inbred and stubborn preferences for its own ways, people are always susceptible to human emotions that can reach them, touch them, and provoke a reaction.

Limping Home from Cannes

In 1991, I had the honor of serving as president of the jury of the Cannes Advertising Festival, the most prestigious and well-attended event among the various annual advertising award shows around the world, celebrating what the judges determine are the most creative examples of our craft. Some critics of the advertising business, including occasional clients, have wondered why such expressions of self-congratulations are necessary. I recall during a pitch for one of the world's most important and coveted global accounts, as we paraded in front of the prospective client the industry-leading number of creative awards BBDO had won, one of the owners of this multibillion dollar company interjected a chilling statement.

"Allen, that's all very nice," went the comment, "but we don't care about awards and we never will. They have nothing to do with growing our sales," he concluded with a note of defiance.

The point was certainly arguable, and in fact, such a debate has gone on for all the years I've been in advertising and is likely to continue for as long as the business exists. But the best explanation I've every heard for why awards are indeed important is actually a good joke.

A little girl thinks she's a chicken. Her understandably

concerned parents have her examined by a psychiatrist who explains that their daughter is probably just going through a phase in which she associates with animals, and that in short order, she will no doubt grow out of it. Her father reacts in horror.

"Doc, that's *terrible!*" he exclaims.

The doctor reassures him that the problem is not threatening and that there is no cause for concern.

"You don't understand, Doc," replies the father, "we need the eggs."

The reason advertising people award each other prizes and trophies for their work is that our egos need the assurance, even if it comes mostly from ourselves, that we are indeed creative, artistic, and capable of reaching people's minds and hearts.

We need the eggs.

So as head of the panel of judges in Cannes, my role was to organize and lead our discussions, resulting in the selection of winners in a wide variety of product and service categories, and to serve as a spokesman to the press, keeping them apprised of our progress and deliberations, stimulating interest and expectations about the potential winners.

My fellow jurors were creative leaders selected from advertising agencies all over the world, a truly international group. While most of us would be meeting for the first time in Cannes, we were all aware of our respective agencies' reputations and credentials. By the conclusion of a full week of day and night judging sessions, we would know each other far better, and in some instances, for worse.

The judging process was well known for being often highly political, with biases among judges who usually supported entries from their respective countries and geographic regions. It was not exactly an objective exercise and in fact, certain regions were renowned for outright conspiracies between their judges, agreeing to support each other's entries while downgrading the work from other areas. As president of the jury, I had no voting power beyond any of the others, but I was determined to see if I could do something to make our panel as fair, impartial, and unprejudiced as possible.

I was actually able to find a way to eliminate outright fraudulent votes while allowing the judges to overtly and openly support their constituencies. The first rounds of judging had been conducted by computer, with the judges entering a score of zero to ten for each entry they viewed. Each judge had his or her own keypad, so the voting was secret. No one knew what score was assigned by anyone else. The computer would provide a printout of the aggregated scores by which we would reduce the many thousands of entries to a few hundred, the top scorers in each category. These would then be the subject of our face-to-face discussions in which we would select gold, silver, and bronze award winners from the computer-generated list of finalists in each category.

Since this first phase of winnowing down the entries was the only time the judges' opinions were private, it didn't take a Sherlock Holmes to deduce that this was where any deals between the judges would be struck to influence the outcome. What they didn't know was that the computerized results would include not just the average of their scores, but also a spreadsheet showing how each of them had voted in every instance.

When the computer produced the results, I sat down for a night with the numbers.

I found absolute and unarguable proof of collusion between particular judges who voted in perfect accord, giving zeros to entries outside their geographies and tens to their hometown favorites. In most instances, their schemes were so blatant, they didn't even have the subtlety to assign various lower scores to what they had determined to eliminate, or different higher numbers to what they wanted to win. Had they been more creative in their scoring, it would have made it much more difficult for me to recognize while trying to scan spreadsheets showing thousands of entries.

With this information in hand, I began our first joint session by informing the other judges of what I had found. I did not name anyone or any of the advertising involved. I simply gave them a choice. We could accept the list of finalists generated by the computer, with all its attendant phony votes, which I would then reveal in detail or we could use an alternative list that resulted from my deleting the scores that had been skewed by the now obvious deceptions. It did not take long for the jury to unanimously vote for the adjusted list.

But our now more honest tally did leave a few judges with the difficulty of having little and in some cases no advertising from their homelands under consideration for an award, which would be apparent since the list of finalists was always made public. So I suggested, and we quickly agreed, that all judges could peremptorily and without objection add two entries of their own choosing to the list. Obviously, such additions would not win awards, but they would satisfy every judge's need to have shown support for his colleagues at home.

The people who ran the festival were delighted to be able to leak to the press that we had counteracted the traditional and predictable plots to influence the scoring, and had developed a revised system that would henceforth automatically do what I had done manually — eliminate the highest and lowest scores during the computerized phase of the judging, thus minimizing the possibility of continued judicial corruption. And having been credited with this initiative, I was feeling pretty good about myself and the ongoing judging.

Until we came to the selection and awarding of the festival's Grand Prix.

The awards at Cannes are in the form of trophies in the shape of a lion. And the Grand Prix was the best of the best, the *one* commercial from among all the winners that stood out above all the rest. You can imagine that it usually produces a fairly lengthy and heated debate among the jurors, certainly true in our case. In fact, we argued between two commercials long into the day of the festival's closing gala at which all the winners are traditionally announced and the lions presented.

When time finally ran out on us, we had selected the Grand Prix by a margin of just one vote, with me in the minority. I wasn't happy with our selection. I believed that compared to the other spot in contention, it was less an example of advertising and too much a case of self-conscious, artsy pretension, with far less of a message that the consumer could either rationally or emotionally understand as a reason to want the brand.

But the vote had been taken, and that was finally that.

All that was left for me to do was make a short speech at the award show, hand out the lions as they were announced, and pose for pictures as the winners came on stage to receive their prizes. The audience at Cannes consists mostly of creative people from agencies around the world who have entered their work and therefore have a vested interest in the results. Given the location in the south of France, they are largely from the major countries of Europe, where it is traditional for audiences to express their pleasure or anger with raucous cheering and applause, or jeers, boos, and catcalls. At Cannes, this mass expression of opinion is carried to the extreme.

As the program drew to a close with the announcement of the Grand Prix, the creative crowd was on the edge of their emotional seats. The award would be accepted by the man who had directed the winning commercial, Jean-Paul Goude, a famous French film director. Clearly, the audience shared my lack of enthusiasm for the winner, because when I called Goude to the stage and a reprise of his film began, the auditorium exploded in a torrent of hissing, whistling (an insult in European theaters), and shouts of derision.

Ordinarily, the winners say a few words of thanks as they receive their trophies, but with the din of abuse cascading from the balcony and rising from the orchestra, Goude chose to express himself differently. He took the Grand Prix (a rather heavy metal casting) from my hands, raised it above his head as though in triumph, but then flung it with all his might to the floor, turning on his heels and stalking away to the even more energized outpouring of scorn from the crowd.

The curtain came down on a scene of pure chaos.

What nobody had noticed, except me, was that the trophy Goude had hurled to the stage didn't actually land on the floor. It crashed down on the top of my foot, which x-rays later revealed caused a fracture of the something-or-other bone, leaving me in considerable pain and with a pronounced limp for many days to come.

I didn't do any celebrating at the dinner that followed. At what otherwise might have been a highlight of my career — president of the Cannes jury, with all the attendant global publicity, the lights and music swirling around me in the full glamour of the Côte d'Azur as the creative community of the advertising world danced away the night — I instead sat glumly with one shoe off, my foot throbbing and swelling, convinced beyond any reasonable doubt that I was in a business fundamentally out of its mind.

The Upgrade

Bruce Crawford preceded me as CEO of BBDO. He left the agency to become general manager of the Metropolitan Opera, eventually taking over as its chief executive. And after successfully running the Met for many years, he later became chairman of Lincoln Center. He now serves as chairman of the executive committee of the Met. And all the while, he kept his hand in the advertising business by returning as chief executive of the Omnicom Group, which he helped build into the industry's largest holding company, and has remained its chairman to this day.

As this brief résumé clearly shows, Bruce has achieved great success in two careers, either of which would be a lifetime accomplishment for most people. He is a person of exceptional intellect, with a variety of eclectic interests even beyond his involvement in the worlds of business, finance, and the performing arts. He loves watching horse racing, baseball, and hockey. His idea of a great weekend is to shop at New York City's fresh food markets, cook what he buys, read, sip a fine wine, listen to music, and watch movies on his home entertainment center. He is truly a Renaissance man with the additional quality of having a poignant, and often quite self-deprecating, sense of humor.

Years ago, it was only because of Bruce that I stayed at BBDO during a particularly stressful period when I seriously thought about leaving. At the time, he was running the company's international division, and I had recently become the agency's creative director. I was considering another job because the previous creative head would not let go of the reins, making my life miserable. Bruce knew this and offered many cogent reasons why I should stay. But none of them had the impact of his closing argument.

"If you leave," he said, "so will I."

His remark shocked me, and for a moment, I didn't know what to say. "C'mon, Bruce," I finally responded, "I appreciate the sentiment, but that makes no sense. Why would you do a thing like that?"

"It has nothing to do with sentiment," he replied. "It's simple. I wouldn't work at an agency that was stupid enough to lose you."

I stayed because even though I knew he had his sights set on running the agency, I believed him. Maybe I just wanted to, but I couldn't imagine a greater compliment, and Bruce was not inclined to offer them gratuitously. Of all his qualities, the last word I would use to describe him is "sentimental."

Eventually, he did head BBDO, and it was Bruce who chose me to succeed him. To say I have great admiration and affection for Bruce, and that I owe him a great deal, would barely suffice.

Finally, Bruce is a man who harbors few illusions about anything in life, least of all himself. But on one particular occasion, one of them caught up with him.

By his own admission, Bruce expects and enjoys being catered to by top restaurants, hotels, and such service organizations frequented by leading business and public personalities. And he always believed that his position in the arts, rather than in advertising, was far more the source of the deference shown him by the maître d's and managers of the many-starred establishments where he ate and slept.

Bruce certainly thought that was the case when he arrived at a posh hotel in Honolulu, where he had stayed a number of times while at BBDO. But this was his first trip to Hawaii as head of the Met. He had reserved his usual executive suite but this time, as he checked in, the manager rushed from his office to welcome him.

"Ah, Mr. Crawford, how good to see you again," he gushed. "I am so pleased to welcome you back," he continued, "and to offer you one of our largest luxury suites. Of course," he added with a flourish, "with our compliments."

"Thank you," Bruce replied, masking his delight with the detachment of someone receiving something fully expected. And so he spent the next few days and nights luxuriating in the oversized, ornately appointed accommodations usually inhabited by the richest and most famous, but this time by the head of the world's most renowned opera company.

Shortly thereafter, Bruce attended a dinner at the White House and was seated with Secretary of State George Shultz and his wife. At one point during the meal, Mrs. Shultz turned to Bruce and thanked him for the favor she said he had done them during his recent stay in Hawaii. In fact, Bruce had no idea what she was referring to, but before his confusion could become apparent, Mrs. Shultz explained.

"We were there in the same hotel as you," she said, "but the security people were very concerned because they wanted someone the management could vouch for to occupy the suite next to us. They told us they would arrange for the head of the Metropolitan Opera to have the suite, and now I know it was you who solved our problem. So," Mrs. Shultz concluded, "George and I want to thank you and apologize for any inconvenience we might have caused you."

"Oh, it was no trouble at all," Bruce replied, laughing as he realized the upgrade he thought had been his due was, in fact, for a far less glamorous reason.

No doubt Mrs. Shultz couldn't imagine what Bruce thought was funny. She had no way of knowing that despite his attendance at this impressive event, joined by the president of the United States among many other dignitaries and heads of state, he was laughing at himself.

The *Gaijin* in the Kitchen

In developing a relationship with our advertising agency partners in Japan, it occurred to me it might be beneficial to bring
my two teenage daughters along on one of my visits. Lizzy had
been studying Japanese to fulfill her language requirement in
high school. Her ability to understand and speak this very foreign language far surpassed the obligatory and rudimentary
phrases I usually fumbled through, so I thought meeting her
would earn some appreciation from my Tokyo colleagues. Her
sister, Laura, spoke the universal language of joie de vivre that
could bring a smile to anyone's face, friend or stranger alike.

The downside of course, was that as teenagers, decorum
was not their primary concern. Compared to us, the Japanese
are very proper people, quite proud of their heritage and society, and polite to a fault in almost every circumstance. Other
than late nights in the karaoke bars, the formal dignity with
which they usually conduct themselves stands in stark contrast
to the American high school scene from which Lizzy and
Laura would be bopping their way into far eastern culture.

But they're both smart kids (if I say so myself), and I
trusted that their appreciation of the opportunity to visit Japan
as part of my need to build the relationship with our people

there would result in at least a temporary moratorium on their usual off-the-wall behavior. I hoped for the good manners and personal restraint that I had explained ad nauseam was expected of them.

Our hosts responded to Lizzy and Laura as I had expected, with enthusiasm that far exceeded their traditional politeness. They were quite taken that Lizzy studied their language, truly thrilled that my daughters would show an interest in their country, and immensely proud that I would want my children to meet them. Beyond arranging for them to spend time around Tokyo with their younger staff members while we held our meetings, they also insisted on planning a day for us in the mountains, where we would stay in a traditional Japanese inn, operated by people well known by our local management.

It was there, and thankfully not in Tokyo, that my carefully laid plans to win the hearts of the Japanese with humility, deference, and unassuming modesty literally almost went out the window.

I was certain that our agency managers had paved the way for our visit by alerting the staff at the inn that I was the head of our company, although their exceptional courtesy and dedication to our every comfort would no doubt have been no less in any case. Any self-consciousness we had at being *gaijins* melted away in the warm friendliness of their welcome. We returned their hospitality by making every effort to show our appreciation by constantly smiling, bowing, and thanking them for every service. Maintaining this level of civility to which we were so unaccustomed also required us to suppress a continuous urge to giggle, which we managed while in the presence of our ever attentive hosts.

As part of our experiencing Japan, our rooms featured the traditional wood and paper partitions, tatami mats, and a dining table only high enough for us to slide our legs underneath, with pillows on the floor as seats. We had a lovely view of woods literally right outside our sliding doors, with a mountain stream below us.

We removed our western-style clothes, changed into kimonos, and went off to enjoy the incredibly relaxing hot baths that literally seemed to drain all tension from your body. We returned to begin the customary multicourse meal served by women dressed as geishas. The menu included a variety of fish and other seafoods, meats, all kinds of vegetables, and some local delicacies that previous trips to Japan had taught me not to ask too much about. In fact, I had warned Lizzy and Laura that there might be a few dishes, some cooked and some not, that they would have to grin and bear so as to avoid insulting our hosts. I advised them that in those cases, it was best to just hold their breath and swallow quickly with little or no chewing.

Early in the meal, however, we were served a rather spongy substance which, after prodding and poking it with her chopsticks, Laura could not resist asking about.

"Excuse me," she began politely, "but what is this dish?"

The server looked at Laura quizzically, obviously not understanding her question. Lizzy haltingly, but apparently accurately, translated. She visibly blanched at the response.

"She said it's an eel. And I'm pretty sure she said it's raw," reported Lizzy.

"No way, Dad," said Laura.

"We'll discuss it when she's left the room," I replied, speaking under my breath through a forced smile. "I told you, Laura, you have to, even if it's just one bite,"

"Can't do it, Dad," she insisted, when we were alone. "Why can't I just flush it?"

"Too risky," I said. "They'll hear it and know what you're doing or maybe it'll get stuck," I went on, now totally paranoid.

"Okay," said Laura, getting to her feet and sliding back the panel door overlooking the brook. "Out it goes."

"Laura, *no!*" I exclaimed.

"Oh shit!" she gasped as she flicked her wrist to send the eel over the side.

"What?" I said, alarmed.

Laura turned to show me her totally empty hand and burst out laughing. "I just tossed the whole bowl in the woods. It slipped," she said, laughing even harder.

"That's just great. Now we're missing a bowl," I said, as Lizzy joined Laura, laughing at my distress.

"It's just a bowl, Dad," said Lizzy.

"Yes, but they'll *know*," I shot back. "The Japanese are very organized, very into details," I practically moaned.

"So, whadda we do, Dad?" asked Laura, still laughing.

"Just sit back down," I replied. "I have an idea."

I crawled up from the table, and made my way out of our rooms and down the hall. I wandered around the inn until I found the kitchen, where a couple of cooks and our serving ladies were working. They stared at me in amazement as I entered, smiling profusely and bowing in every direction, pretending to be interested in their preparations, but all the while glancing around to find where they kept the dishes. When I finally located the shelf with the bowls, I slowly worked my way over to it while continuing to look with great intensity at the foods being prepared nearby. I delivered one more deep and smiling bow to the cooks and ladies, and turned to leave while blocking their view of the stack of bowls. I snatched one off the shelf, stuck it in the sleeve of my kimono and headed back to our rooms.

"Ta da!" I announced in triumph, sliding back the door to our dining area, holding up the pilfered bowl. Laura took one look and started laughing, as I regaled them with my exploits.

"You stole a bowl?" Lizzy exclaimed in disbelief when I had finished my recitation. "And you're worried about the impression *we're* making? You know what, Dad?" she continued. "You're really crazy."

I couldn't argue the point.

Now You See Them, Now You Don't

In the mid-'80s, Roger Enrico, on his way to eventually becoming the chief executive officer of PepsiCo, took over from John Sculley as president of the Pepsi-Cola division of the corporation. John had left the company to become head of Apple Computer. He is an extremely smart man, highly organized and disciplined in his thinking, which tended to be linear and process driven. Roger is equally bright, but far more instinctively reactive and creatively oriented in his approach to marketing.

Almost immediately, Roger issued a challenge to our agency and to Pepsi's head of advertising, Alan Pottasch. For the preceding twenty years, Alan and BBDO had worked together to create some of advertising's most beautiful and emotionally appealing commercials for Pepsi, under the theme of "The Pepsi Generation." Alan became known as "the father of the Pepsi Generation," a recognition we always kidded him as alluding more to his age than his marketing acumen. In fact, Alan is one of the most perceptive and creative clients BBDO has ever served, and to this day, after well over forty years, continues to influence our work on the Pepsi brand.

"The Pepsi Generation" slogan was intended to signify that Pepsi was the drink of a special group of people, youthful in spirit regardless of age, and dedicated to getting the greatest enjoyment out of life and the freedom to pursue their own paths. The commercials were filmed and edited to inspire the viewer, usually with a song and musical accompaniment that would reach right to the heart.

Unfortunately, over the years, Coke was able to evoke a similar response with their advertising, which was sometimes equally evocative, moving, and more effective by virtue of their larger advertising budget. Roger felt Pepsi advertising had to change. It needed to differentiate itself from Coke, re-state its greater relevance in people's lives, and do so in ways that would not ring true for Coke if they tried to emulate our approach.

Roger wanted a new campaign and he devised a brilliant way to get it started.

He signed up America's hottest star in popular music, the singer at the top of the charts, month after month, song after song, album after album — Michael Jackson. He paid Michael what was then an almost unthinkable five million dollars to appear in just two commercials for Pepsi. Then he turned to Alan and Phil Dusenberry, head of creative at BBDO.

"Make it happen," he ordered.

We created and produced one commercial that was a choreographed street scene of kids imitating Michael and his chorus of singers and dancers, only to discover Michael actu-ally performing with them. Another spot featured a concert setting with Michael on stage in front of a screaming audience. (This was the famous production in which Michael's hair was burned by fireworks that had been set off to dramatize his entrance, but that's another story.) Both commercials featured a rewritten version of Michael's hit, "Billy Jean," that he had adapted to Pepsi's message.

A few weeks before the commercials were to break on-air, Pepsi launched a barrage of publicity to stimulate what turned out to be unparalleled news coverage of an advertising campaign, all focused on the new commercials starring "the king of pop" pitching Pepsi. It began with a news conference at the famous Tavern on the Green restaurant in Manhattan's Central Park. There, in front of cameras from network and local TV news programs, Michael appeared with Roger as the new advertising was introduced.

As if Michel himself wasn't enough, his managers had arranged that the master of ceremonies presenting Michael to the assembled reporters would be Don King, the ubiquitous boxing promoter, famous for his ability to turn even a pre-fight weigh-in into a news event.

That was the scene — King, flanked by Michael and Roger, the room packed with Michael's people, Roger's people, King's people, and of course, BBDO's people, among the assembled reporters. The television camera lights blazed as King began by singling out all the sports and entertainment celebrities in the audience. He waved toward the back, screaming, "*Tommy Hearns,* middleweight champion of the world is here. Hey, Tommy, great to see ya!" He then pointed off in another direction. *"Sammy!* It's Sammy Davis, Jr. Thanks for comin', Sammy!" He turned to the other side of the room, pumping his fist, yelling, "*Reggie Jackson,* Mr. October, here from the New York Yankees to be with us!" And finally, throwing both arms in the air, King reached a fever pitch, pointing over and over to the back of the room with both hands as he shouted at the top of his voice, "And right there is the greatest, the greatest heavyweight in the history of boxing, *Muhammad Ali!* Yeah! Yeah! Yeah!" King exulted.

Everyone in the audience was turning and craning their necks toward the back of the room to where King was waving and pointing. But it was impossible to see anything beyond the blinding lights and bulky cameras set all around the perimeter of the area.

What no one except King knew was that not one of these superstars was actually there. No Tommy, no Sammy, no

Reggie, and certainly no Muhammad. The audience couldn't see past the lights and cameras, which was just as well because every one of these delusions of King's grandeur simply *wasn't there.*

But before anyone could figure that out, and with the perfect timing of the consummate con artist, King immediately thanked all the phantom personalities, announcing that they all had to leave for other engagements. Then, with a dramatic flourish, he turned to Michael and brought the audience's full attention back to the podium with an introduction that must have had even Michael blushing behind his ever-present aviator sunglasses and surgical mask.

Michael waved, left the podium, and the press conference was over.

But the real show had just begun. For the millions that Pepsi had paid Michael, the news coverage of their new advertising was estimated to be worth many times more in free publicity and exposure of the commercials. Roger's mission to distinguish Pepsi from Coke would be accomplished in ways that for years to come would help Pepsi overcome the distribution and marketing budget advantages that Coke enjoyed.

And to this day, as I think back on the chaos of that press conference with all the personalities announced by Don King but not actually in attendance, and as I review in my mind's eye the image of Michael, his face covered by sunglasses, breathing mask, and the brim of his huge black hat, saying nothing and offering no more than a brief wave of his arm before quickly disappearing from the scene, I find myself wondering whether it's possible, just possible that . . .

It couldn't be. Could it?

The Bialystock Method
of Time Management

In many service businesses in addition to advertising, clients are usually very concerned with how much attention they will receive from the top management of the company, specifically from the CEO. This comes first from the reasonable, though not necessarily realistic assumption, that people in the leadership positions of a company, starting with the chief executive, can offer the highest level of intelligence, insight, and innovation in providing solutions to the clients' problems. And second, it is a matter of ego — purely and simply the notion that clients want and need to believe that they are so important as to warrant being the personal concern of everyone up to, and particularly including, the chief executive.

The fact that a CEO might actually have somewhere between little and no knowledge about, or involvement in, the workings and offerings of his or her company (as has become the legal defense of choice among the indicted) never quite overcomes the ego's demand for recognition. Thus, when seeking to win a client's business, a CEO in a service industry must always prepare for the question of how much personal time he or she will devote to the account.

Of course, the instinctive and probably most truthful answer is: "As much time as you need." Unfortunately, that is not what clients want to hear since it leaves their egos totally unsatisfied. The somewhat less ambiguous version of that answer, which goes something like: "Certainly a disproportionately large amount of time as we get things going, which can then taper off to whatever we need to insure things continue to go smoothly" also does little to advance a client's ego gratification.

No, what the client wants is a number — a quantified percentage of the CEO's time. Now certainly no one would believe anything near fifty percent since even the most ego impaired business prospect would have to conclude that the CEO isn't working very hard on the company's other businesses, or he has proved to be of little value to them. And you can be equally sure that something around the more likely number of twenty percent will not be heard as a clarion call of commitment.

You might conclude that the question has no good answer. Which brings us to Max Bialystock.

For those who have not seen either the film or the stage version of Mel Brooks's classic comedy, *The Producers,* the lead character is Max Bialystock, a bankrupt Broadway producer who concocts a scheme to offer every investor *fifty percent* of a new show he is touting, obviously intending to have far more than just two investors. In effect, he sells the show many times over. And he expects to get away with this scam by putting on a production so terrible that it will close immediately, eliminating any expectation of anybody getting any money back. It's a brilliant scheme provided that nobody knows how many fifty-percent shares have been sold and, more important, that the show is indeed an opening night flop.

It didn't quite work out for Max, but it did provide an opportunity to deal with the time management conundrum regularly put to us by our clients. The litany would go something like this:

"Well, Allen," the client asks, "just exactly how much of your time can we expect to have on our business?"

"Let me answer you," I begin, "by first explaining that at BBDO, we do not subscribe to the Bialystock method of time management," a declaration which invariably results in blank stares. "I'm sure this is not something you ever heard of in business school, so let me be more specific," I continue, launching into the tale of Max Bialystock and how he conjured up his ploy to fleece investors. "The point is," I say in ending the story, "that most CEOs will tell you — and every one of their other clients — that they will devote a big percentage of their time to your account. It's like Max Bialystock, and you don't have to do the math to know that doesn't compute, even if they are working a twenty-five-hour day, eight days a week, thirteen months a year. I don't play that game," I say, denigrating my competition with just a hint of self-righteousness. "I can't give you a number," I continue, "but I can assure you that I'll know what we are doing for you, I'll tell you what I think whenever an important decision is being debated, and I'll be there when you call. And," I conclude with perhaps a dab of defiance, "I have no idea what percentage of my time that will take."

That did the trick almost every time. Because in fact, it wasn't a trick at all. It was an innocuous way of suggesting that the question the clients were asking, and the answer they were looking for, were unrealistic.

For that, I owe Max Bialystock. Unfortunately, it's a debt I can't repay. But I'm sure he would understand.

The Business We've Chosen

During the course of creating advertising for our clients' products and services, BBDO has had many occasions to recommend the use of famous people from the entertainment world as spokespersons and/or endorsers of brands. Generally, the more popular the personalities involved, the more complex and difficult the negotiations. Eventually, we have to deal with talent agents, personal managers, financial advisors, friends, and flunkies offering unsolicited and gratuitously fawning advice. And it is usually no easy matter to handle the insatiable egos of the stars themselves. Finally, the legions of lawyers representing both the client organization and the celebrity's interests compound the complexities by requiring everything to be spelled out in excruciatingly minute detail.

Even then, when you thought there couldn't possibly be anything left to discuss, the deal could still be derailed by something totally unexpected. This was the case when we once attempted to enlist a very famous entertainer whose name was regularly emblazoned among the lights of the Las Vegas hotel marquees.

After months of starts and stops, stating and restating, doing and undoing, the deal was done. We were sure of it. The money, the shooting date, the media plans, the cancellation and renewal terms, the scripts, the ancillary activities that would complement and help promote the advertising campaign, the clauses explaining the clauses that explained everything that could, or would, or might occur in conjunction with the production of the commercial and its subsequent use — all of it had finally been agreed.

Or so we thought. A few days before we were scheduled to shoot the spot in a Hollywood studio, our lawyer got a call from their lawyer.

"We have a problem," said the star's lawyer. "He can't be in Hollywood on the day of the shoot."

"What are you talking about? You guys signed off on everything," replied our lawyer.

"Well, there's a wrinkle that's come up in the contract we have with the hotel where he's performing" said their lawyer. "It seems that during the run of the show, he can't travel outside Vegas without their expressed permission."

"C'mon," said our lawyer, "you can't be serious. L.A. is less than an hour away."

"Well, maybe that's why they'll okay it," replied their lawyer, "but they've gotta say so. You know who these guys are who run the hotels, and there's no way we're gonna mess with them. In fact," he went on, "if we have even a prayer of getting this done on time, I think your man needs to see Carlo Barzone (an alias for this story). Him and a bunch of other guys with *similar names,* if y' know what I mean," he said, pausing for emphasis, "own the hotel. But he's the capo-whatever-they-call-it. He's not gonna talk to you or me, but these guys are always looking for angles, so I'm guessing he'd take a meeting with the head of a big ad agency. We can try to set it up, but your guy's gotta carry the ball," he concluded.

That's how one day later, after a hastily arranged trip to the West Coast, I wound up on my way to the San Bernardino Valley for an appointment at four o'clock in the afternoon at the home of Carlo Barzone. There I was, head of a major international company, with a mission to convince a reputed mafioso to allow a big-name entertainer to spend a day in Hollywood shooting a commercial. When I had told a friend in New York about why I was making this sudden trip, and whom I was seeing, he laughed.

"I'll bet he shows up in his bathrobe and slippers," he said.

I thought that was just stereotyping until I rang the bell of a large, gaudy house, on what appeared to be a property spanning more than a few acres. The door opened, revealing a portly figure wearing slippers and a bathrobe with the mono-gram "CB," holding a cigar in one hand and a drink in the other. I stifled a wry smile and introduced myself.

"Yeah, I know," said Barzone. "C'mon in." As I followed him into the foyer, replete with marble floors and a five-foot-high fountain, he said, "Why don't we go sit by the pool? Whaddaya wanna drink?"

"Maybe just a Perrier," I replied, then quickly correcting myself, "or better yet, a San Pellegrino."

"So you run this ad agency, BB-somethin'-or-other?" asked Barzone as we sat on the veranda overlooking his heav-ily stoned terrace and opulently landscaped pool.

"BBDO," I replied. "It stands for Batton, Barton, Durstine, and Osborn," I said, and for some inexplicable rea-son added, "but they're all dead."

Barzone looked at me with a peculiar expression as if to say, *Hey, relax. I wasn't gonna kill 'em.* "So what's on your mind?" he asked.

"Oh, didn't they tell you why I came to see you?" I replied, surprised.

"Yeah, this lawyer said somethin' about a contract an' some trip I had to approve, but I never listen much to those jerk-offs."

I explained the situation and as I finished, Barzone cocked his head and looked at me quizzically. "Your business must be kinda slow. You came all the way from New York just to ask me *that*?" he said in amazement.

"Well, the lawyers thought it was a good idea since you have the right to prevent our talent from traveling away from Las Vegas."

"What a bunch of assholes," Barzone exclaimed. "Fuckin' shysters drive me nuts. Whaddo I care if the guy goes to L.A. as long as he's back in Vegas in time to do the show?"

"That's no problem," I said. "We'll see that he is."

"Yeah, I bet you will," said Barzone. "You wouldn't wanna be owin' me for all those ticket refunds. Hey, ya wanna stay for dinner?" he added suddenly. "I wouldn't mind learnin' a little about the ad game."

I thought I'd better quit while I was ahead, and I felt that the longer I stayed, the less likely I'd wind up that way. I certainly didn't want to encourage Barzone and associates getting involved in the advertising business. So I thanked him for the invitation, told him I had to catch the next flight back to New York, and headed for the door.

As he opened it to let me out, he said, "Hey, d'ya know the difference between somethin' bad and somethin' terrible?"

I wasn't sure what he was getting at and thought maybe he was going to leave me with a parting threat to insure that his headline act got back to the hotel in time after the shoot.

I answered a little tentatively, "Uh, no."

"It's *bad* when a planeload of lawyers goes down in flames," he said. "It's *terrible* when ya find out there wuz a few empty seats."

I laughed. Barzone laughed louder. "Fuckin' lawyers really wasted your time," he said. "Ya coulda just called me."

As I stood there watching him tuck his bathrobe around his waist and shuffle in his slippers back into the house, it wasn't just this farcical day that I was wondering about wasting. I was thinking about all the months, all the meetings, and all the money that so many of us were putting into producing — what? A commercial.

And as I drove away from casa Barzone, I remembered a line, appropriately enough from *The Godfather,* spoken by the Hyman Roth character as he lectured Michael Corleone about the need to accept the ironies and frustrations of their dealings and their lives.

"This," he said, "is the business we've chosen."

The Last Supper

In 1986, less than a year after I became chief executive of BBDO, we began merger discussions with two other advertising agencies, Needham Harper and Doyle Dane Bernbach. But these were no ordinary negotiations, since the merger we contemplated would be unique in the history of the business. Usually, two companies would come together to form a larger and ostensibly stronger single entity. We were *three* agencies looking for a way to unite, each with its own specific reason for no longer wanting to go it alone.

In our case, BBDO had gone on the stock exchange in 1973 in order to raise capital for global expansion. But by the mid-'80s, American business was in the throes of merger mania with companies in every industry acquiring each other to form fewer and larger enterprises. Growing a business organically by beating the competition had become growth by buying your competitor's business and assimilating it as your own.

Saatchi & Saatchi, the most voracious acquirer in advertising, had become the world's largest agency, buying companies almost randomly and usually for far more than they were worth. The Saatchi brothers, Maurice and Charles, seemed to have practically unlimited capital available from banks indiscriminately eager to lend them money, and they were never hesitant to issue more shares on the London exchange to raise even more money to pay for their purchases. As a British company, they had some significant accounting advantages over American agencies to the point where they could outbid U.S. buyers and seduce reluctant sellers with offers beyond even their own exaggerated ideas of their worth.

As a public company, BBDO was vulnerable to such tactics, which we thought might be irresistible to our shareholders but would result in the end of our brand and our plans to build it, just at a time we felt we had developed both the talent and financial strength necessary for future success.

Needham was a smaller agency than BBDO and, being privately owned, did not have the financial wherewithal to expand globally. As a predominantly Midwestern American agency, their competitiveness would clearly suffer in the inevitable globalization of client businesses. They needed to merge with someone, and like us, felt threatened by the prospect of acquisition by the Saatchis. In Needham's case, it would probably have resulted in losing their identity entirely in an eventual forced merger with some other Saatchi agency.

And for Doyle Dane Bernbach, the issue was more one of near-term survival. DDB had begun a downward spiral from prior years of great success during which they had gone public, and after a series of management changes, now faced disgruntled shareholders only too eager for someone to offer them a premium for their shares. They needed to be acquired, so much so that for them, the Saatchis represented more of an opportunity than a threat.

Indeed, even as we and Needham worked with DDB to create our three-way alliance, they were secretly in talks with the Saatchis to sell them the agency. This is what precipitated a highly dramatic and even more chaotic scene on the last night of the negotiations that would finally result in the creation of Omnicom as the new holding company for BBDO and what would become DDB Needham, a combination of those two companies. We had painstakingly agreed on the valuations that would result in the conversion of our respective equity into new Omnicom shares. The boards of both BBDO and Needham had approved the deal, but DDB had repeatedly asked for more time to convene their directors. Now they were finally meeting, as the two other agencies and our investment bankers gathered in my office to await the vote of the DDB board.

It was only then that we learned their board was considering an alternative offer and that Maurice Saatchi was literally sitting outside their boardroom also waiting for a decision after presenting his offer. My office broke into bedlam. Everyone talked over everyone else, all of us furious that DDB had blindsided us, and at the same time, speculating on what we could do to defeat the Saatchi offer. We now knew their price for a DDB share was higher than the value of the Omnicom conversion that a DDB shareholder would realize. But another critical difference was that our deal had no conditions attached. Once accepted, the price could not change. However, the Saatchi offer involved performance parameters which DDB management would have to achieve over time, or else the price would ultimately be discounted. Finally, above all the shouting, someone posed the critical question.

"Should we offer more money?"

That brought the room to order. In fact, to dead silence.

"That's the question, all right," I said, "and it's now or never. But keep in mind," I added, "that we'd have to go back to our board for approval. And I'm not gonna do that unless our investment bankers go on record right now as to how much more, if anything, is financially feasible."

It was almost worth all the angst caused by DDB's last-minute bombshell to see the analysts break out in an instant sweat. And indeed, they were on a very hot seat. If they recommended that we increase the DDB conversion ratio, and subsequent returns did not justify it, they could be culpable. But if they advised us to hold firm, then the deal, and millions of dollars in fees, could be lost. So they hemmed and hawed with "what if's" and "maybe's" punctuated by the furious punching of their calculator keys as they crunched the numbers for the various assumptions of any new offer. Finally, they had an answer.

"We can't see offering any more," they glumly announced as their verdict.

"Okay, that's that," I said. "Call the DDB boardroom and find out what's going on."

A few moments later, the head of our investment banking team put his hand over the mouthpiece of the phone and whispered, "Their board is recessing for dinner and they'll talk more when they get back. Is there anything you want me to tell them?"

I believe people who know me would agree that I don't usually act on impulse or in anger, but now I had reached my boiling point. This was the last night for negotiations because we had all agreed that any substantive leaks about our deal would mean we would have to deny it, and in fact call it off, since it would cause horrendous disruption among the clients and the agency staffs. All I could see was DDB playing fast and loose after two months of intense day-in-and-day-out discussions, not to mention the impact of their antics on the future welfare of BBDO and Needham. Before I even thought about the consequences of an ultimatum, I issued one.

"You tell those sons of bitches there's no more time for their stalling," I exploded at a wide-eyed and stunned investment banker. "If they leave for dinner, tell 'em they can have a nice, big meal and take their time to enjoy it, 'cause we won't be here when they get back. Tell 'em they've got fifteen minutes to make a decision," I finished in full rant, "or we're outta here and the deal is off!"

Really, I'm not nearly that tough. We waited almost an hour in a state of absolute anxiety before they called to tell us their board had approved our three-way deal and their merger with Needham.

As a postscript to this night of nuttiness, our deal actually exacerbated the Saatchis' desperate drive for dominance. I used a pretty good line in our announcement interviews, which turned out to be a harbinger of their next move.

"Omnicom is now the biggest advertising company in the world," I said, "but knowing the Saatchis, that probably won't last much more than ten minutes."

This proved an accurate prediction because very shortly thereafter, they bought the Ted Bates agency, a very large transaction that we knew from our own investigation, cost them at least twice what it was worth.

A few weeks later, I ran into Bob Jacoby, head of Bates, who reputedly took home over a hundred million dollars for his shares.

"I think you owe me fifty million bucks," I said to him.

"What the hell are you talking about?" he shot back.

"Well, if we hadn't done our deal and become number one, the Saatchis would never have paid you double for your agency," I replied.

"Maybe you're right," he said. "Send me a bill," he added, and walked away laughing.

But Maurice and Charles Saatchi didn't have too many laughs after that. Their deal to buy Bates eventually proved to be the acquisition that broke their financial backs. Their dreams of glory eventually turned into nightmares of shareholder rebellions, lawsuits, and management acrimony that resulted in them finally losing their company.

Ironically, the Saatchi & Saatchi agency survived and today does very well. But without the brothers whose name it bears. Maurice and Charles also continue to enjoy the good life. But without the agency they created.

Et Tu, Mr. President?

In addition to my job at BBDO, I have worked since 1986 for
the Partnership for a Drug-Free America, an organization dedicated to using advertising to help reduce drug use, especially
among teenagers. We believe that if advertising can motivate
and persuade people for the purpose of selling them something, then advertising ought to have the corollary ability to
"unsell" a product or point of view. So we've worked toward
that goal with measurable success over the years, enlisting the
services of advertising agencies who have volunteered their
creative and production capabilities to develop magazine and
newspaper ads, TV and radio commercials, billboards and
posters, and more recently Internet communications, all designed to make drugs less attractive to young people.

At one point, through the efforts of Jim Burke, the former
head of Johnson & Johnson, and then chairman of the
Partnership, we were able to enlist the first President Bush to
tape a commercial supporting our anti-drug campaigns. Jim
was a friend of the first lady, Barbara Bush, who had personally appeared at Partnership events and who, at Jim's request,
had asked the president to do the commercial. He would give
us fifteen minutes in the White House at nine o'clock on a
Monday morning.

However, on the Friday before the scheduled taping, Mr. Bush suffered some sort of irregular heartbeat. With the president in the hospital over the weekend, we got the news that our Monday morning session was canceled.

Until early Monday morning. My phone woke me a few minutes after six.

"I just got a call from the White House," said Jim. "The president left the hospital a few minutes ago and he wants to do our commercial as originally planned."

"You mean at nine this morning?" I asked incredulously.

"Yeah," Jim replied.

"They've got to be kidding, Jim," I said. "That's less than three hours from now."

"Yeah," Jim replied.

"Well, how the hell can we get there in time? The last time I looked," I said, "the Concorde doesn't fly from New York to Washington."

"I'm already there," said Jim ignoring my wisecrack. "I have another appointment in Washington this morning, so I came down last night. They'll have a White House camera crew ready to go at nine o'clock sharp."

"Great," I said. "Put the script on cue cards, tell the camera man to point it at Bush, and get him to read it in less than thirty seconds."

"Allen," said Jim with the weariness of a parent talking to a spoiled child, "you're our creative director and he's the president of the United States, the leader of the free world, ready to do your commercial against drugs for the benefit of kids all over America. Do I really have to deliver a speech to get you out of bed, on the shuttle, and over to the White House as fast as you can?"

Jim was a gentleman whom I never heard curse and never saw lose his temper or his cool in a crisis. He was the man, after all, who made the unhesitating decision to remove every tablet and capsule of Tylenol, his company's largest seller and most profitable product, from every store in America as soon as he learned that someone had poisoned a few packages.

Despite his measured wording, I got the urgency of his message. As someone less temperate would have put it, *Quit bitching, get the hell out of bed, and get your ass to the White House.* Which I actually did, arriving shaved, showered, and fully dressed, beating the president by two minutes to the room set up for the taping.

When we had finished, Mr. Bush turned to Jim and me. "Listen fellas," he said, "my schedule for most of this morning was canceled since I was in Walter Reed Hospital for this heart thing, so I'm free for a while. How about a cup of coffee in the Oval Office?"

There's a joke about President Kennedy agreeing to say hello to some salesman so he could impress his customer. When the president comes over and says, "Hi, good to see you again," the guy says, "Not now, Jack, can't you see I'm busy?" For a split second, it was so tempting. *Sorry, George, can't do it. Gotta get back to my office. I'll catch you for coffee some other time.*

Of course, I kept my smart-ass, New York liberal Democrat mouth shut except to respectfully thank the president for his invitation, as I followed him to the Oval Office. And I admit that sitting there, sipping coffee served by a U.S. Navy steward and chatting casually with the president of the United States, overcame every bit of both my natural and practiced cynicism.

During the conversation, Jim said to Mr. Bush, "Mr. President, the Partnership is very grateful for your time this morning, but could I ask you for one more favor?"

"Well, Jim, you can certainly ask," said Mr. Bush with a smile. "What's on your mind?"

"I was hoping, Mr. President," Jim said, "that maybe the next time you make any comments about the drug problem, you could put in a good word for the work the Partnership is doing, for the people who work there, and for all the volunteers in the advertising industry who give us their time and talent for free. It would be a great thing for all these people to hear a few words from you about this."

"Okay," Mr. Bush agreed, "I'll make a note of it and pass it along to my speech writers." But then, just as he began to write, the president looked up from his desk.

"You know, guys," he said, "everyone around here tries to get me to do what *they* want me to do. And the writers all try to get me to say what *they* want me to say. Sometimes I think they're all having a contest to see how often they can avoid doing what *I* want. So I have to warn you that just because this note comes from me makes it a pretty sure thing that it probably won't get done."

Wait a minute, I thought, *did I really hear what I thought I heard, coming from the president of the United States?* I assumed the same thing happened often enough to Jim at J&J, just as plenty of people at BBDO played those kinds of games with me as I tried to manage the company. I'm sure we both understood exactly the nature of the complaint. But I nevertheless found it quite disconcerting to hear it from the man who had just said it.

I suppose in retrospect I should have known better. I should have known that the president of the United States does not wield nearly the power the office portends. Like most chief executives, he just can't compete with the bureaucrats who manage and manipulate the systems. The federal government has just too many bureaucrats and too many systems for even the president to get control of them.

So I guess the presidents and I will just have to accept it as the way of doing business in our respective enterprises. At least we get pretty good perks.

The Boss's Wife

In 1979, I married Missy Weston-Webb, a television producer who worked at BBDO. Her legal name is Suzan, but when she was a child, her mother had a maid who called her "Miss Sue." Her baby sister pronounced it "Missy," and it stuck.

The agency had a policy against hiring married couples but no prohibition against a husband and wife working together when they married after becoming employees. I'm not sure about the rationale for this distinction, but in any event, it did not prevent something of a contentious issue from developing between us.

Coincidentally, fourteen years earlier, my first wife and I were both being interviewed at BBDO. And we were both offered jobs, she as a market researcher and I as a copywriter. Since the agency would hire only one of us, we decided that since she did not consider the advertising business a probable career, while I did, I would accept the job.

Due to the apparent anomaly in the agency rules, this should not have been a problem for Missy and me as newlyweds. But within a few months of our wedding, it was.

It happened right after my promotion to president of the headquarters agency in New York. Tom Clark, who ran our agency in Detroit, where we worked for Chrysler, came to see me. Tom was a very astute executive, quite well attuned to the politics and idiosyncrasies of our business.

"I need to talk to you about a personal matter," he began.

"Do you have a problem?" I asked.

"No," he replied with his usually impeccable timing, "*you* do."

"What are you talking about?" I asked, thinking that I hadn't been president for very long and already I had somehow screwed up.

"I'm talking about you and Missy," Tom replied. "She's gotta leave the agency."

I wasn't sure whether to be relieved or even more concerned, knowing how much Missy enjoyed her job. "Well, I checked the policy, Tom," I said, "and it doesn't say anything about —"

"It's not the policy and you know it," said Tom, seeing right through my feigned denial. "You know damn well the wife of the president of the company shouldn't be working here, especially in a paranoid business like ours. People are watching their backs enough without this," he went on. "It's just gonna make everyone uncomfortable dealing with her."

"Yeah, I know that. You're right," I conceded. "So why don't *you* go talk to her about it," I said with a wry smile.

"Hey, I went through the same shit with Karen," he said, referring to the fact that his wife had also been with the company when they married. "You're on your own, pal."

A few days later, over dinner and an almost finished bottle of wine at one of Missy's favorite restaurants, I broached the subject.

"There's something we have to discuss," I said with just a hint of an ominous overtone, figuring that if she thought I would suggest something alarming, she might accept a relatively unthreatening situation with greater calm.

"Don't tell me you're pregnant," she laughed, completely undoing my little ploy.

"Ha, ha," I replied. "This is serious," I said, pausing dramatically in an effort to regain my lost psychological ground.

"What's the matter, are you sick?" she asked, finally showing some real concern.

Gotcha, I thought. "No, it's nothing that serious," I replied. "It has to do with you working at the agency."

"What's the problem?" she asked, her narrowing eyes showing her on full alert.

I can appear ingenuous when it suits my purpose, but Missy really is. "Well, a number of people have suggested," I said, extrapolating Tom's talk with me to include those who wouldn't have had the guts to say it, "that it's not appropriate for you to work at BBDO now that I'm president."

She thought about it for a nanosecond. "Bullshit," replied my beloved.

"C'mon," I said, "how can you expect people to deal with you honestly when you're married to the guy who can promote them or fire them? They're gonna watch everything they say around you. Worse yet, they're gonna bullshit you."

Missy cares greatly about openness and sincerity in her personal relationships, but she just wasn't buying the argument.

"I'm just a TV producer," she said. "It's not like I have any influence on the business. What's the big deal? You know I like what I'm doing and you also know I won't get into another agency with you running BBDO," she continued, which was, of course, true.

"Well, people at BBDO are just gonna tap dance around you every time you're in the room. They'll never be straight with you," I said, playing my last card. I knew that to fall back on any suggestion about propriety or the appearance of nepotism would carry no weight with Missy and worse, it might make me look like a wimp in her eyes.

"I'm not worried about it. Let's get the bill," Missy said, strongly suggesting an end to the discussion.

"Okay, okay," I agreed. I appeared to give up, but only because I had just gotten an idea that I felt certain could convince her that working for BBDO had become untenable.

The next morning, I went to see our head of TV production, Missy's boss.

"I'd like you to do a little survey for me," I told him, without mentioning that this had anything to do with Missy. "I think it's important for us to be sure we've built teams of people who really like working together," I said. "In your department, for example," I continued, "if the TV producers don't have the confidence and trust of the account executives, it will be very hard to get them to sell our production budgets to their clients. So I'd like you to ask the account head in charge of every client to designate their top three choices of TV producers they want to work with, so we can plan the best match-ups. But whatever you do," I warned him, "don't tell anyone that this came from me. Tell them it's just for your planning purposes. And let me see the results before you do anything," I concluded.

About two weeks later, he came to my office with a chart showing even more emphatically what I had expected. Every one of the account executives running our various client businesses ranked Missy as one of the top three producers they wanted to work with. Not one of the dozen or so other producers shared that distinction.

"See anything peculiar?" I asked him.

"Looks like there's a lot of sucking up going on here," he replied. "Is that why you had me do this?"

"Yep," I said. And I told him about my talk with Missy. "She's never even met half these guys and they're falling all over themselves for her."

"Well," he said, "at the risk of being an ass kisser myself, she's damn good at her job and I'd hate to lose her. But you're right. She shouldn't stay."

"Thanks," I said. "I may ask you to repeat that to her if I can't convince her this time."

But he didn't have to talk to her. And neither did I. All I had to do was show her the survey. She looked down at the paper. She looked up at me. She saw exactly what I'd done and why I'd done it.

"You're a miserable, sneaky bastard, and I don't want to work in your company any more. I quit," she said, handing me back the survey like it was used toilet paper. "But no other agency will hire me because of you, so what the hell am I supposed to do?"

"You could have a kid," I suggested.

"With whom?" she archly responded.

In fact, we eventually had two girls, and Missy devoted herself to them and to my two sons from my first marriage. She also became involved in a variety of charitable endeavors immediately after leaving BBDO. And she turned into a tennis fanatic. I haven't taken a set from her in the last ten years.

Ironically, shortly after her pseudo-voluntary retirement, she said, "You know, I don't think I would ever want to go back to work. But don't get me wrong," she added, before I could suggest she thank me for my successful survey scheme, "you're still a miserable, sneaky bastard."

Of Men and Mice

When BBDO became the advertising agency for Tambrands, the company best known for the Tampax brand, their chief executive was Martin Emmett, a rather prim and proper, eastern-establishment type. He was tall and slim, impeccably groomed, and elegantly dressed, with quite the look of someone Hollywood might have cast as a top Wall Street lawyer or financial executive. Martin struck me as belonging very much in the trappings of his office, highlighted by the obviously expensive heavy wooden desk and bookcases, with upholstered chairs and sofas sitting on what I'm sure were authentic Oriental rugs.

But at the same time, he looked almost laughably out of place among packages of the various forms, sizes, and shapes of the Tampax product line, prominently displayed everywhere around him.

Soon after winning the account, we were summoned by Martin to discuss the latest innovations in Tampax products and how to best communicate them to consumers. It was a lunch meeting in Martin's office, with sandwiches and beverages wheeled in on mahogany serving carts and distributed around a large coffee table to the assembled group. In addition to Martin and the BBDO team, it included the head of

Tambrands research and development, the Tampax marketing vice president, and their advertising director.

The incongruity of Martin's patrician presence among the Tampax was just the beginning of this incongruous scene. Because there, in the middle of the table, among the roast beefs on rolls, the ham-and-cheeses on rye, the pickles, chips, sodas, and coffees, sat an oddly shaped test tube next to a beaker filled with blue water, and a variety of unwrapped and unsheathed tampons. To add a crowning note of absurdity, there was not one woman among us for what was obviously going to be a graphically detailed conversation about Tampax and its role in helping women through the menstrual cycle. Regardless, as the research scientist reached for the test tube, signaling an end to the lunch part of the meeting, we wiped the crumbs from our lips, folded our non-sanitary napkins, and went to work.

"Gentlemen," he intoned, unwittingly reinforcing the idiocy of the moment, "this device has been custom molded to replicate the average size and shape of the female reproductive organ." It occurred to me that he intended to conduct this entire meeting without once using the word "vagina," as indeed he did.

"The blue water you see in front of you," he continued, "represents what we call 'the flow,' which is the menstrual fluid or discharge." I further realized that he also wasn't ever going to use the word "blood," which indeed he didn't. At the moment, I didn't grasp the enormity of his achievement. Carrying on a discussion of menstruation while completely avoiding those two words was the linguistic equivalent of describing a baseball game without using the words "base" or "ball."

"The water is blue," chimed in the advertising director, "because the networks do not allow us to show the flow in red in any of our commercials."

Well, if it isn't blood, why should it be red? I thought, but did not say aloud.

"What I want to demonstrate, gentlemen," began the

researcher again, "is that the rate of absorption and the ability of the material to retain the collected fluid, in terms of both quantity and length of time, are superior in Tampax products compared to our competition. Watch," he commanded, his eyes literally lighting up with anticipation as he proceeded to insert a tampon into the organ-shaped test tube. He poured a measured amount of blue water into the top of it, pausing to allow the tampon to absorb it. Then, with fingers poised below the lower opening of the test tube, he delicately grasped the string on the end of the tampon and withdrew it, holding it aloft.

"The mouse," he announced triumphantly, "has not leaked a single drop."

"The *mouse*?" I asked incredulously.

"Well, that's our nickname for the tampon," he explained somewhat sheepishly, "because of the little tail on the end that women use to pull it out. But," he added with a little giggle, "we don't call it that in our advertising."

"Of course not," I said. "Women are afraid of mice."

Without showing the slightest appreciation of my remark, he then repeated the experiment numerous times with various other "mice," holding up each in turn by its tail to prove the same successful result. When all the "mice" had been suitably drowned and laid to rest in front of us, Martin asked the question I had begun to fear was coming.

"So, do we have something here we can advertise?"

"Do, uh, your mice always hold, um, more fluid than the other guys' mice?" I asked, fighting to keep a straight face.

But before anyone could answer, our account executive intervened, sensing that I had crossed the line, approaching a giddiness not likely to inspire the client's confidence in the agency.

"Why don't we look at all your lab test results, check with the networks as to what they will allow us to show given the sensitivity of the category, and then come back to you with a recommendation?" he suggested.

Everyone agreed that was the right next step and so the meeting ended. But there would not be too many more for BBDO or Martin Emmett at Tambrands. As it turned out, we and Martin both lacked the necessary feminine insight, understanding, and experience that market research alone could not provide.

All of us men were eventually replaced without ever achieving any notable success in the manufacture and selling of "mice."

He Ain't What He Used to Be

One of my responsibilities as head of BBDO's worldwide enterprise was to seek alliances, mergers, or acquisitions with companies in disciplines related to ours. I would sometimes meet with people who owned and/or ran marketing oriented firms specializing in such fields as public relations, direct mail, telemarketing, entertainment and events, custom publishing, and in recent years, interactive communications. One such meeting took place in London, where I sat down one afternoon with David Simmons (his name has been changed to protect his sensibilities), head of a large and well-established international network.

We thought we could expand our services in helping clients build their brands by linking our advertising activities to other marketing communications programs that could deliver our clients' brand messages in parallel with our media campaigns. David shared our belief that advertising and his specialty were different but essentially complementary tactics to accomplish the same objective — to reach diverse but sometimes overlapping client audiences through a variety of communications channels. We saw his work as part of a package of integrated services we could sell to clients. He in turn saw us as providing access to a longer list of larger and more multinational clients that he might otherwise not be able to reach through his offering alone.

We talked for an hour or more about the possibility of bringing his company and BBDO together in some sort of co-ordinated structure. It did not take long for us to agree on the merit of the idea, but we realized that we would have much more to negotiate since David's intent was to sell BBDO his company, continue to run it, and have a meaningful position in BBDO's management group. None of these were excessively ambitious or unwarranted expectations, but each, particularly the price, required detailed and defined specifics as to how it would be handled. With this in mind, we agreed to schedule further discussions.

It came as no surprise to me to learn shortly thereafter that David was having similar meetings with my counterparts at a number of our competitors. Obviously, he was shopping for the best deal he could get, especially the price he would be paid for his shares. I assumed, however, that he would also have been concerned with the quality, character, and culture of any potential partner, criteria in which I thought BBDO had many advantages to offer. In fact, I naively believed his interest in them would at least to some extent mitigate what I soon discovered was his expectation of an excessive share price, a result of the unrealistic frenzy of merger and acquisition activity going on in many industries.

This was the mid-'80s, a time of merger mania fueled by junk bonds and share offerings, some of it based on the legendary schemes of the infamous Charles Ponzi, in which the negative results of one bad investment would be temporarily hidden by a subsequently larger but usually worse purchase. It was a decade in which the price paid to buy a company was almost no object, and doing the deal was more important than worrying about a reasonable return on the investment.

As one of our bankers put it, David was playing "dialing for dollars," the hottest game in business in those days. Indeed, even before we had arranged a second meeting, another advertising agency answered his call with an offer no one could refuse. And so we had no reason to meet again.

Many years later, I was returning from a trip to London, awaiting my flight in the Concorde lounge at Heathrow Airport. I hated the Concorde, and only flew it because its speed and the time change between the two cities meant you'd arrive in New York more than an hour earlier in local time than when you left London. The plane was noisy, with aisles so narrow you had no chance to get to the lavatory once the serving trolleys were out. And if you were lucky enough to beat them to it, you found yourself in a space so small you had to literally bend over while bracing yourself on the wall or ceiling with your one free hand to maintain your balance. The seats in the cabin were so cramped it was impossible to use your tray as a desk, so getting any work done was not an option. Just getting to your briefcase underneath the seat in front of you required the agility of a contortionist. There was at least time to read, uninterrupted by any movie since there was none, but only by the periodic blather from the cockpit about the superior supersonic design of the aircraft. And all this was yours for a premium of only about twenty-five percent more than the subsonic, but still astronomical, first-class fare. It cost about six thousand dollars *one way* by the time Concorde was mercifully retired from service, having run out of spare parts, and despite its price, without ever achieving even a dollar of profit.

Seated next to me in the lounge was a very nattily attired, distinguished looking gray-haired gentleman, whose British enunciation would have made Henry Higgins smile with pleasure. I could hear him speak alternately on the phone, apparently to business associates, and to the lounge attendants, who seemed to fuss inordinately about what he might like to eat or drink. He peaked my interest because he looked vaguely familiar. But I couldn't place him.

When we boarded the plane, I found myself seated next to

him in the first row of the first cabin. I had this seat only because of a last minute cancellation. In addition to the various wonders of flying on the Concorde, it was a status symbol to be seated closer to the front. Since all seats on the Concorde cost the same and tended to arrive at their destination simultaneously, I can only assume that the only real benefit of a seat assignment closer to the door was the speed with which you could escape the Concorde's discomforts.

As my mysterious traveling companion handed his suit jacket to the attendant, I distinctly heard her ask, "Is there anything we can do for you before take-off, Lord Salisbury?" (This peerage name is also an alias.) Since I didn't know any Lord by that or any other name, I stopped wondering about him looking familiar and thought no more about it.

While the captain carried on about "the slight nudge you will feel as we activate our reheats to propel our aircraft through the sound barrier, thus achieving supersonic speed," I opened the book I was reading, *The Brothers: The Rise and Rise of Saatchi & Saatchi,* about Maurice and Charles Saatchi, who had achieved considerable notoriety in advertising. They had built one of the industry's largest companies by acquiring many other firms through the excessive and ultimately disastrous use of equity and borrowed funding. Having met them and even negotiated with them on a few occasions to no conclusion, and being familiar with many of the companies they had acquired, I was curious to see how they and their deal making were depicted. I found the book an unjustifiably adoring treatment for what soon after became an enterprise that collapsed under a mountain of debt and hubris.

After a few pages, I heard the mellifluous voice of Lord Salisbury.

"Forgive me but I couldn't help noticing what you're reading. I actually know Maurice and Charles quite well and I'm rather curious as to how you find this book about them."

"Well," I replied, conscious of trying to improve my usual

New York syntax and diction, "it seems to me, it places them on a pedestal that rather quickly crumbled."

"Yes, of course," he said. "By the way, aren't you Allen Rosenshine?"

Whoa, wait a minute! I exclaimed to myself. *His Highness, the Duke or Baron of something-or-other knows me?*

"Uh, yes, uh, I am," I answered, somewhat flustered.

"Yes, I thought I recognized you in the lounge at Heathrow. I'm Lord Salisbury."

"Pleased to meet you," I said, "but how did you —"

"You don't seem to remember that we've met before," he interrupted with a clear hint of annoyance.

"I'm sorry," I said. "I must admit, I'm at a loss."

He paused for a moment, looking at me slightly askance. "Well, actually, I used to be David Simmons," he said, with absolute solemnity and not the slightest trace of irony.

I had no doubt he was serious. All I could think of was, *In what business but advertising, with whom but a salesman in the House of Lords, and where but the Concorde?*

The Hanging Curve

In the early days of baseball on television, BBDO had the American Tobacco Company as a client, creating the advertising for their Lucky Strike cigarettes. For many years, they and another client, Schaefer Beer, were the major sponsors of the Brooklyn Dodgers, and so our executive in charge of those accounts, Tom Villante, spent a great deal of time with the team, organizing and supervising the television and radio commercials during the broadcasts of their games.

As it turned out, Tom and I had a few things in common besides both working at BBDO for many years. We have the same birthday, March 14, which Tom always reminded me we also share with Albert Einstein, a point of absolutely no significance regarding either his or my intelligence. We grew up in adjacent neighborhoods in New York City, we both went to the same high school, and were reared by parents of modest means but sufficient to afford us a comfortable, college-educated upbringing. We were both sports enthusiasts with dreams of playing professional baseball that certainly surpassed our abilities. And of course, we both wound up in advertising.

But Tom had far more of a fun job because of his assignment to produce advertising on the Dodger games. Each year, he would go to Florida for spring training with the team, spending time with them in Vero Beach as they prepared for the coming season. And when the games went from exhibitions to the regular season, Tom was at Ebbets Field in Brooklyn for all the Dodger home games, and traveled with the team back and forth across the country on their road trips. He was as close to living the life of a major league baseball player as you could come without ever putting on a uniform or taking the field.

Over the years, he became almost a member of the team. He was welcome in their clubhouse, and became friends with Dodger players and many of their opponents. He spent many hours with the Dodgers during the long trips to other cities, in those days often by train, and was with them during the days and nights between the games away from New York and their families.

This was how, as Tom explained to me some years later, he became a very good gin rummy player, certainly the best I ever met. We were once flying back from Chicago after a trip to our Quaker Oats client, when he broke out a deck of cards and casually asked me if I wanted to play some gin. I knew how to play and thought the game far more a matter of luck than skill. But after losing practically every hand to Tom over the next two hours, I realized he knew quite a bit more about the game than I did. When I asked him how he had become so good at it, he told me he had passed much of his time on trips with the Dodgers playing gin rummy with them, augmenting his agency income by beating them regularly, but only for modest amounts since he didn't want to jeopardize their friendship. (He did not afford me the same courtesy, so I've never played with him again.)

At the end of spring training, it was traditional for the Dodgers to play the New York Yankees in the teams' final exhibition games. Those were the days when the now San Francisco Giants also played in New York, and the three teams featured arguably the three best centerfielders in the game — Duke Snider, Mickey Mantle, and Willie Mays. Sports fans in New York constantly argued about which of them was better than the others, but one thing was not open to debate — Snider had no success batting against Whitey Ford, one of the Yankees' great pitchers. Ford could throw a wicked curve ball, and even when Snider knew it was coming, he simply couldn't hit it. Almost every time Snider would come to the plate, Ford would throw three curves for three strikes and Snider would trudge back to the dugout.

On one trip from Florida to New York, where the Dodgers and Yankees would play their exhibition series, Tom and Snider were playing gin. In the middle of a hand, as Snider was thinking about what to discard, he looked over at Tom, who had his fingers pressed against his forehead, mumbling some words with his eyes closed as though praying.

"What the hell are you doin', Villante?" demanded Snider, annoyed that he was, as usual, behind in the score.

"Hey, Duke," said Tom very innocently, "it's nothing. It's just a thing I do to help me play."

"What are ya talkin' about?" asked Snider.

"Look, Duke, I shouldn't tell you my secret, but I use mental telepathy when I play gin. That's how I beat you guys all the time."

"I'm gonna ask ya one more time, Villante," said Snider, this time with a menacing note in his voice, "what are ya talkin' about?"

"Okay, Duke," Tom replied, "you probably won't believe me, but I'll tell you how it works. Whenever I need a particular card, I try to get you to give it to me by using the power of suggestion, sending a message from my brain to yours. Like I concentrate real hard and I think over and over in my mind, *Throw the five of diamonds, throw the five of diamonds, throw the five of diamonds.* And most of the time, you give me the card I'm looking for."

"What a crock of shit," said Snider.

"Well, whatever you say, Duke, but look at the score," Tom responded. "Listen, I'll tell you what," he continued before Snider could get even angrier. "Tomorrow, you know Ford is gonna pitch for the Yanks, and you can't remember the last hit you got off him, right?"

"Yeah, thanks for remindin' me," said Snider petulantly. "What's that got t' do with playin' gin?"

"Well, listen to me," Tom went on. "Try mental telepathy on him. Try the power of suggestion like I'm telling you."

"How?" asked Snider tentatively, his curiosity at least a little peaked.

"Before you get in the batter's box, concentrate the way I do. Keep repeating to yourself over and over, 'Hang a curve, hang a curve, hang a curve.' If you do it before every pitch," said Tom, "maybe it will get through to him and he'll hang one." (Villante was referring to the fact that when a pitcher "hangs a curve," it means that instead of the pitch bending very sharply as it comes toward the batter, it hardly curves at all, and seems to "hang" in the air so it can be easily hit.)

"C'mon, Villante, you gotta be shittin' me," said Snider.

"It's up to you, Duke," said Tom, "but what d' ya have to lose?"

The next day, Tom was sitting in his usual seat in the Dodger broadcast booth to coordinate airing the Lucky Strike and Schaefer commercials between innings. He watched as Snider walked slowly toward home plate to bat against Ford. Just before he stepped into the batter's box, Snider asked the umpire for time out and stood with his fingers touching his forehead, obviously mouthing some words.

The Yankee catcher, Yogi Berra, looked up from his crouch behind home plate.

"What the fuck are ya doin' Duke?" he asked in astonishment.

Hang a curve, Snider mouthed silently before turning

to Berra. "Shut up, Yogi," he said, "I'm *thinkin'*. But you wouldn't know shit about that, would ya?"

"Yeah, Duke, I don' think about hittin' the ball, I just do it," Berra replied. "Get your ass in the batter's box an' we'll give ya somethin' t' think about."

Ford threw his first pitch, a curve that started out toward Snider's head and broke sharply over the plate.

"Stri-i-i-ke one," intoned the umpire.

Snider stepped back, raised his hand for another time out, reached for his forehead and repeated his incantations before getting ready for the next pitch.

"Yer lookin' good, Duke," said Berra. "You keep thinkin' about it 'cause here it comes again."

Ford threw another curve that had Snider backing away as the ball curved even more than before.

"Str-r-r-i-i-ike two," called the umpire, a little more dramatically.

"Hey, Duke, didja see that?" taunted Berra. "Nah, I guess ya missed it while you wuz busy duckin'."

Again, Snider stepped back, jaw clenched and grim-faced as he put his hand to his head and this time mumbled the words over and over almost audibly.

"Hang a curve, hang a curve, hang a curve."

Berra lifted his catcher's mask and stared at Snider. "Whaddaya, fuckin' nuts?" he exclaimed.

Ford delivered yet another curve. But this time, Snider was determined to hit it. He swung with all his might, missing completely as the ball broke down and almost into the dirt.

"Ste-e-e-erike three," yelled the umpire, signaling Snider's strikeout out with a flourish.

"Way t' go, Duke," said Berra, laughing.

"Fuck you, Yogi," snarled Snider, turning toward the dugout. Then he raised his middle finger toward the broadcast booth and started screaming, "Fuck you, too, Villante. You're a dead man."

Tom survived Snider's threat by demonstrating convincingly that mental telepathy worked, if not on the baseball field, at least at the card table. All that season, Snider beat him at gin rummy almost every time they played.

Just Another Tom, Dick, or Bill

Wrigley, the world's largest maker of chewing gum, has been a family-run company since its inception. Today, its chief executive is the son of the Wrigley who headed the company when it became a BBDO client. His name is William Wrigley, Jr., and "Bill" is what he likes people to call him. His father, however, was called "Mr. Wrigley" by all his business associates without exception, even when he was not present.

We acquired the Wrigley account when we purchased the Arthur Meyerhoff agency in Chicago, where Wrigley is headquartered, not surprisingly in the Wrigley Building, one of the city's landmarks. It was Meyerhoff's only account but Wrigley's market leadership, its size, and its prospects for global expansion made the acquisition especially attractive to us. Our growing worldwide resources and depth of talent brought Mr. Wrigley's blessings on the deal. BBDO Chicago, bolstered by the Meyerhoff purchase, thus became Mr. Wrigley's advertising agency.

For all his personal wealth, his high standing in the business community, and his position in running a major corporation that far and away led its category, Mr. Wrigley did not wear his fame or fortune on his sleeve. His office was not excessively large, nor were its appointments in any way lavish. His small frame was an almost ironic counterpoint to his corporate stature. He shunned personal publicity, and were it not for the fact that his name was in thousands of stores, on millions of packages, on a major league baseball stadium, and listed on the New York Stock Exchange, you could have been introduced to him without getting the slightest hint that you were meeting one of America's most prominent businessmen.

While he may in private have been more authoritarian than consensus oriented in the management of his company, the only outward suggestion of his corporate power I ever saw from this otherwise polite, soft-spoken, shirt-sleeved, almost self-effacing man was that everyone called him "Mr. Wrigley."

Even though he met with us fairly regularly and did not hesitate to let us know what he thought of his advertising, our work and our people were far from Mr. Wrigley's top priorities. So it was with some surprise that I learned from our Chicago group that Mr. Wrigley wanted to spend a day at BBDO headquarters in New York reviewing the status of his brands and meeting more of the agency people involved with his business.

After making a comprehensive presentation, we suggested he might like to meet some of the staff who had not participated in our discussions. We suggested the more casual setting of the after-hours bar we operated in the agency, a place for employees to gather and relax at the end of their day.

The relatively unstructured informality of an advertising agency was not a business milieu to which Mr. Wrigley was accustomed, which would be compounded by the even more relaxed atmosphere of our bar. Yet he seemed, in his outwardly humble fashion, willing to do it. So we gathered the people from our research, media, and other related departments including writers, art directors, and producers who supported our Wrigley marketing and advertising programs, and we took Mr. Wrigley to meet them.

Of course, they had all been briefed that they were to refer to him in the manner to which he was accustomed.

Everything appeared to be going very nicely amidst the wine and cheese. Mr. Wrigley was introduced all around, shook everyone's hand, and chatted amicably with practically all the people in the room, each of whom religiously maintained the protocol of how to address him. The words "Mr. Wrigley" were clearly the most often used over the course of the cocktail hour.

Those of us who had spent the day with him tried not to monopolize the conversation since the idea was for him to get a sense of the number and variety of people who contributed to servicing his business. But at one point, Mr. Wrigley made his way over to me and asked me to step out of the room with him. I thought at first that he might be too shy to ask a stranger where to find the bathroom, but when he asked, "Could we talk privately for a moment?" I heard the first alarm bell of an otherwise successful day.

"Of course, Mr. Wrigley," I replied. "I'm sure we can find an unoccupied office if that's okay with you."

"That would be fine, Allen," he said. "I have a problem that's been troubling me that maybe you can help me correct."

Now my warning sirens were going full blast as we walked down the hall looking for an empty office. *He's got a problem. He's troubled,* I thought. *He says there's something I have to correct.* My mind raced through the subjects we had talked about over the course of the day, trying to think of where we might have gone wrong. *Damn, and I felt it had all gone so well,* I thought, as we stepped into a vacant office.

"I've been embarrassed in there," he said as soon as I had closed the door. *Ah shit,* I thought, *someone in the bar must have called him "Bill."*

"Well, I'm really sorry, Mr. Wrigley," I apologized. "I hope nobody got too familiar —"

"That's just it, Allen," he interrupted. "It's your people calling me 'Mr. Wrigley' all the time. All these advertising people I just met must think I'm a real stuffed shirt. I suppose someone must have told them to do that," he said, "but it's really making me uncomfortable."

Being greatly relieved to learn that we hadn't screwed up the business, I unfortunately did not stop to think before I responded.

"Well, uh, *Bill*," I replied, "why don't you just ask everyone not to?"

From the sudden, sharp look he gave me, I realized I had just completely missed his point. I understood, a moment too late, that his complaint was only his way of telling me, *I know people in agencies are on very familiar terms with each other and probably address their clients by their first names, so I don't want them to think less of me because I am called "Mr. Wrigley,"* which was, of course, exactly what he wanted to be called. And I had foolishly responded, *Okay, I'll call you "Bill" and you should tell everyone else to,* which was not at all what he had in mind.

So he just shrugged his shoulders and we headed back to the bar. And while it turned out that Mr. Wrigley had no problem with what he had seen and heard from BBDO that day, I was left wondering whether that also included me.

I know that Mr. Wrigley was, after all, a gentleman because he neither commented on my lack of perception nor seemed to hold it against me in future meetings.

But to this day, I have to think twice about calling his son — even though he is young enough to be my son — "Bill."

The VW and the Jeep

In the early '70s, BBDO acquired majority ownership of a large and successful agency in Düsseldorf, and I was on my way to Germany for a visit to nurture the new relationship. As I took my seat on the Lufthansa flight, I began the inevitable rumination of a first generation American Jew on an unaccustomed trip to the Fatherland.

That fat guy across the aisle looks like a typical bürgermeister, I thought, *and he's about the right age. I wonder what he did in the war?* Of course, my speculation went well beyond just that relatively innocent question. What I really meant was, *"How many of my relatives could he have killed in the concentration camps?"*

Both my parents had emigrated to America from Poland after the First World War, leaving behind members of their families who later perished in the Holocaust. I vaguely remember as a child that my father had returned to Poland after the war to search for survivors. But he found none. So my survey of the possible war criminals traveling on my flight continued, fueled by the combined forces of historical fact and paranoid fantasy.

As the plane crossed the Atlantic, I slept fitfully, being surrounded by potentially lethal enemies of my people. But I took some comfort from the defeat of the Aryan *übermenschen* and the subsequent judgments at Nürnberg, and I tried to put such unproductive, not to mention unproved, thoughts out of my head.

One of the principals of our new German subsidiary, Willi Schalk, met me at the airport. Willi is about my age and was therefore not personally a subject of my dark speculations. He speaks English fluently and during my visit proved himself a polite, hospitable, and attentive host. And as I soon learned, while he is exceptionally intelligent and fully capable of understanding the most complex business scenarios, his literal German mind allows him to understand a joke, but not necessarily to catch the more subtle implications of a wry remark.

Willi was an early convert to the theories of globalization, popularly advanced by Ted Levitt, a professor at Harvard Business School. Levitt promoted the notion, along with himself, that technological advances in communication would shrink the globe to the point where more and more products would find markets in more and more of the world, with brands able to transcend the limitations of geography and the biases of different cultures. His seminal example was a hypothetical wristwatch that could sell anywhere in the world, since everyone used it for the same rational reason — to know the time. But people would also psychologically appreciate the status afforded by the watch as a symbol of technology and branded designer styling. Levitt dramatized this assumed phenomenon by describing the prospect of otherwise poverty stricken African villagers wearing, along with their tattered clothes, the globally promoted watch. He further extended this marketing model to include a multitude of other products and services, suggesting that ultimate economies of scale would make it feasible, if not competitively necessary, for marketers to expand their sales territories regionally and eventually throughout the world.

While Levitt has been proved largley right, his forecast

ignored the onslaught of the social problems and economic inequities of globalization, as well as the national and cultural imperatives that remain impervious to commerce, ultimately revealing problems he had never considered. As an ad man, I have to admire his eye for staging and publicity in spite of his subsequently admitted excesses on behalf of his product, which turned out to be less the concept of globalization and more the consultancy of Levitt, Inc. (But who am I to condemn the success of a fellow promoter?)

Having spent a few days with Willi and having realized his total belief in the coming of globalization, I found an example of the new paradigm that I thought he would appreciate for its ironic twist. I had noticed when he first picked me up at the airport, that he drove a Jeep. As he took me to catch my plane back to New York, I told him the paradox that had just occurred to me.

"Willi," I announced dramatically, "do you realize that you're driving a Jeep, and that I drive a VW?"

"Ja," replied Willi. "So?"

"Willi," I said, a little incredulous that he didn't seem to get it, "in just one generation after the war, here I am, a Jew from America who drives a Volkswagen, the car Adolf Hitler personally endorsed. And here you are, a German driving a Jeep, the very symbol of the American army that left most of your country in rubble."

"Ja, you are right," said Willi. "Ze VW and ze Jeep are perfect examples of globalization."

Willi remains to this day a good friend whose ability to absorb, process, retain, and act on marketing information, I have always found extraordinary. But I knew then that his dedication to marketing was total, leaving little time for anything such as history, religion, sociology, or psychology, much less the vagaries of the human condition, to interfere with his world view of advertising and his complete focus on our company's growing global business.

This in turn led me to two assumptions. First, I felt that Willi's incredible single-mindedness would benefit BBDO in the years to come. And second, I concluded that his tunnel vision was more a case of compulsion.

The future proved me right on both counts. His workaholic fervor helped build BBDO into a worldwide entity, and was a driving force in the creation of Omnicom and BBDO's role in it. But he also allowed his almost obsessive commitment to business to seriously damage his health, causing him to retire from the company at just past the age of fifty.

Then, after a long period of recovery, Willi threw himself back into the ad business, proving that the creative people in advertising have no monopoly on its irrational behavior.

Unreal Estate

In the mid-'80s, BBDO was in essence evicted from the premises it had occupied for decades on Madison Avenue between forty-sixth and forty-seventh streets. Our lease had expired, and the owners, who had just recently bought the building, would not renew it. They intended to tear down the existing thirteen-story structure and replace it with a high-rise office tower. So one of my major responsibilities as the new chief executive of the company was on a subject — New York City real estate — in which my knowledge and experience fell somewhere between little and none.

Along the way, I was told that at one point during the 1950s, BBDO had been offered the chance to buy the building in which we rented. It would have cost about ten million dollars. Thirty years later, the new owners had paid ninety million. You don't need to know much beyond simple arithmetic to understand that we had passed up a very lucrative investment. That, of course, suggests the story was true, an assumption which I knew at least enough about Manhattan real estate to take with a large grain of salt.

(Many pundits have classified the idea of "truth in advertising" an oxymoron. I would argue the point. However, the concept of "truth in real estate" is not debatable. There isn't any.)

The reason we had chosen to rent rather than buy was expressed in ten words by Charlie Brower, chief executive of BBDO at the time. Having a penchant for the pithy expression, Charlie was reputed to have said, "We make ads. We don't know shit about real estate." Although in this instance, that ultimately proved to be an unfortunate financial decision, many companies would have done far better over the years to have heeded Charlie's advice to avoid pouring money into ventures about which they knew nothing or next to it.

In any event, we had to move, which involved me in a series of meetings with many of the colorful characters in the city's real estate scene. The people I ultimately dealt with ranged from moguls to mobsters, with sometimes little to distinguish between them. Some were convicted criminals. Some would later become guests of the government in less than luxury accommodations. Some practiced real estate's ancillary skills of graft, bribery, and blackmail surreptitiously enough to avoid prosecution. Some stayed within the letter if not the spirit of the law, but usually managed to push the ethical envelope to package proportions. And some were able to maintain themselves above the fray, achieving the goals all of them had in common — wealth (if not actual, at least on paper), power to command attention from the politicians, the press, and the public, and a place in whatever passes for the higher society of the city. They are typified by the man who most personifies their profession, the master of egomania, personal promotion, and dubious claims of net worth — Donald Trump.

But my memorable moment in real estate was not shared with "The Donald," as the media idiotically refers to him. It came from another real estate mogul, probably much wealthier than Trump when all is sold and done, certainly more intelligent as evidenced by his public utterances, and depending on your definition, far classier based on the women he wears on his sleeve. But it was a phone call that proved, regardless of his other qualities, when it came to real estate, he could run with anyone along the low road.

"There's someone on the phone who wants to talk to you about our move," said my assistant. "He says his name is Mort Zuckerman."

"Are you sure he said *he's* Mort Zuckerman or did he say he works for Mort Zuckerman?" I responded skeptically.

"No, he said, 'tell Allen it's Mort Zuckerman calling.' "

I knew him as the owner and publisher of *U.S. News and World Report,* as a well-publicized socialite of New York City and the Hamptons on Long Island, and according to the gossip columns, as a companion of Gloria Steinem, the most prominent advocate of woman's rights. I also knew he was one of the city's major real estate developers. But I certainly didn't know him as "Mort."

"Hello, Mort," I said, not wanting to give him the upper hand in first-name calling.

"Allen, I'm calling you personally because your company is behaving very badly in our negotiations for space in one of my buildings," said Mort. This didn't surprise me since I had hired someone to represent us who was very experienced in doing such deals, and who I was sure could sink to at least the same depths of deception and deceit as any prospective landlord.

"What have we done to upset you, Mort?" I innocently inquired.

"Listen, Allen," he replied, "your people said you want space in one of my new buildings. I have allocated that space. You said you wanted to be the only advertising company in the building. I have turned down other agencies looking for space," his litany continued. "We had a deal, and now I hear you're backing out."

I was surprised, since no recommendation had yet been made to me for any particular building. "Well, I haven't heard about the deal, Mort," I said. "What's the price?"

"That was the only thing left to negotiate," he answered.

Wait a minute, I thought, *is he telling me we had a deal but we hadn't agreed on the price? Does this guy think I'm stupid?*

"Mort, forgive me," I said, "I know I'm not in your league when it comes to real estate, but next to the top three criteria being location, location, and location, would I be wrong to think that the next three are price, price, and price? If we're not agreed on the price, how could we have a deal?"

"Well, your people have walked away from the table. I'm sure we can settle on a price," he replied, petulantly and obviously ignoring my question.

So we re-established the negotiation. But it was clear they wouldn't accept less than a premium price we knew we couldn't possibly afford. And that was the end of that.

I never heard from Mort Zuckerman again. But he taught me a lesson about real estate. You can be a publisher of major media. You can be a celebrity among the social set's glitterati. You can party with Arianna Huffington all over Washington, and in your townhouse in Georgetown. You can be part of the world of fashion and design, with Diane von Furstenberg on your arm. But when it comes to real estate, you'll always be as much of a huckster as any of us in advertising.

Michael, the Martyr

The story of Pepsi-Cola hiring Michael Jackson to appear in their commercials at a time when he was far and away America's, and maybe the world's, top entertainer has been well documented and reported. So too has the fact that during the filming of one of the first spots to run, his hair was burned by some special effects of fireworks. But from the moment the first spark hit the first hair on Michael's head, a series of events behind the scene and under the radar of rationality were set in motion. As if the madness it took to get to the point of actually shooting the spots had not been enough, the accident took it way over the top.

For those of us at Pepsi and BBDO involved in the development of the campaign, it was one of those events about which you always remember where you were and what you were doing when you heard about it. I had been scheduled to be in London on that day but had cut short my trip to return to New York to attend a dinner to celebrate the closing of a deal that would make BBDO the first agency to become a majority owner of a Japanese company, bringing that critical market into full partnership within our global network. We were at the very posh Four Seasons restaurant with our new Japanese colleagues when the maître d' brought a telephone to our table, informing me that I had a call. This was before there was a phone in every pocket and was for me, quite unusual. So I knew before picking up the receiver that it couldn't be good news.

"Allen," said Phil Dusenberry, our head of creative, who was in Los Angeles supervising the production of the Michael Jackson commercials, "I am calling to inform you that fifteen minutes ago, an accident on the set injured Michael and he is right now being wheeled on a stretcher to an ambulance to go to the hospital."

Now I knew the bad news but I was further alarmed by the stilted formality of Phil's message. It sounded like he was reading a statement prepared by a lawyer, as would in fact be the case for almost every public comment by anyone about the incident thereafter.

"What happened?" was my less formal reply.

"I can't go into it right now," said Phil in hushed and hurried tones. "We have to go with him to the hospital. But apparently, he got too close to some fireworks or they went off too soon and his hair caught fire. I don't know how serious it is, but I'm letting you know because this will be all over the news in a matter of minutes and you may get a call from reporters in New York."

"Okay, I'll make no comment since I'm not actually on the scene," I said. Then, in an effort to lighten things up, I added, "Tell me one thing, Phil, did you get the shot?"

He wasn't amused.

And neither were our Japanese guests, who understood little of this conversation but must certainly have thought it rude, since as far as they were concerned, I was conducting other business during our dinner. I knew that explaining the situation would require details that, with the necessary translations, would take us past dessert and were so bizarre that they could not have resulted in much understanding anyway. So I simply apologized as best I could, probably leaving them with the impression that their new partners were impolite, unbalanced, or both.

Phil was right about the press. When I got home later that night, my wife told me a reporter from the *New York Post* had called. I didn't return the call, but nothing anyone could have said would have mitigated their predictably sensationalist front-page headline the next morning.

EXPLOSION INJURES ROCK STAR FILMING TV COMMERCIAL

Below it was a photo of Michael being wheeled into the hospital. By that time, however, we had learned that Michael's wound was superficial, that he would soon go home from the hospital, and that his father had told Phil not to worry because, he said, "It wasn't serious." Shortly thereafter, Michael would fly to New York to appear at a previously scheduled event, with a small bandage on his scalp, making jokes about wearing a Jewish yarmulke.

Meanwhile, an accompaniment of craziness was tuning up for the inevitable legal dance to follow. The television networks were offering top dollar for the film from the commercial showing the accident, which sparked a battle over who actually owned the footage. Was it Pepsi who would ultimately pay for it, or BBDO as their agent, who in fact wrote the checks? Was it the production house that shot the scene, which had not yet been delivered or paid for? Or could it have been Michael himself or his organization, since they had contractual rights of approval for its use, which had not yet been given? In a rare example of good sense and judgment, all the parties at least agreed that the networks should not get the film regardless of who legally owned it.

But at the same time, Michael's lawyers demanded custody of the footage to provide evidence against whomever they were surely salivating to sue, planning that no doubt began the moment he was being wheeled from the stage to the ambulance.

But as they started to build their case for damages, their ardor was considerably dampened by the fact that in addition to any lack of physical incapacity, over the next few days, sales of Michael's albums skyrocketed, earning him millions of incremental dollars clearly as a direct result of the accident, and certainly making it easier for him to endure the mental pain and suffering they were ramping up to claim.

It was the lawyers and management at Pepsi who ultimately put an end to the frenzy. With the injury to Michael being minor, they correctly reasoned that all the publicity attendant to the accident would generate exceptionally positive interest in the commercial itself and Pepsi advertising in general once the spot was completed and about to go on air. And indeed, the commercial was eventually featured on news broadcasts nationwide, providing many millions of dollars worth of free advertising for Pepsi. So they agreed to make a major contribution in Michael's name to a hospital, in return for putting an end to all legal discussions and disputes. Pepsi would look magnanimous, Michael could play the martyr for a good cause, and we could all get back to business.

In retrospect, no one was hurt, and in fact everyone benefited from the accident, so much so that the standard joke ever since has been that BBDO probably *planned* it that way.

But we are neither quite that crazy nor even close to that clever.

The Doctor Will Not See You Now

It should not surprise anyone who has worked in or with an advertising agency that many of its employees — in particular, the creative people who write, design, and produce the commercials and ads — are very insecure. That is largely because an advertising agency does not produce a widget or device with a functionality that can be measured by whether or not it works.

Advertising is essentially an *idea* — the result of someone's thinking. Therefore, when it is deemed good or bad, it is really the *people* who thought of it, shaped it, and produced it who are being judged. Thus, the writers, artists, photographers, film producers, directors, and editors, cannot help but feel personally applauded or attacked when their work is positively or negatively criticized. Their state of mind is always in the eyes and ears of the beholder. They are brilliant or they are boobs because other people think so.

Creative directors — the people in advertising agencies who are ultimately responsible for the work on which their clients spend many millions of dollars — are understandably not known for their consistency or stability of mood. At any given moment, most all their psyches can be plotted somewhere on a psychological grid running from torpor to hyper on one axis, and from naive to mistrustful on the other.

In truth, there are often good reasons when they tilt toward paranoia. As the saying goes, "It's hard not to be paranoid with everyone always doing things behind your back." Most clients, knowing the emotional fragility of their agency counterparts, tend to do everything possible to avoid direct confrontation with creative sensibilities when they are less than enamored with the work. Few will ever come right out and say they just don't like it.

"There's a lot of good work here," they might say. They mean: *There is a lot of work here, but not much of it is good.* "Why don't you leave it with us so we can think about it," they would suggest, meaning in fact: *Why don't you go away so we can figure out how to tell you we don't like it.* "This is really exciting stuff, but it may be too out of the box for our top management," they sometimes conclude, which roughly translates to: *This work is so weird we have no idea what it means.* And even when their enthusiasm seems real, even when they say things like: "This is great, we love it," the odds are good that within a few days, they will find reasons for their ardor to cool.

This syndrome explains the wisdom of two words of advice once offered to me by a veteran of the business when I returned from a client meeting to report that our work had been greeted with great enthusiasm.

"Celebrate *instantly,*" he said.

What keeps creative people coming back for more is that now and again, we find a client who actually says he hates what he hates, and alternately has us produce what he says he loves. And every once in a while, the brand, the market, the consumer, the client, and the agency creative people fall into perfect alignment, and an advertising campaign truly achieves icon status in the minds and hearts of America, as well as on the bottom line of the client.

The rest of the time, it's mostly a wrestling match between the worlds of the figurative and the literal, and you can only brain-slam people a certain number of times before they begin to lose their senses. The more creative a person is, the more likely it will happen.

They are a psychiatrist's dream.

So it hardly raised my eyebrow to learn that one of our best creative talents who for years had undergone the wrenching rigors of accolades on one day and rejection on the next, enjoying the outpouring of praise for successful campaigns and the wrenching recriminations for marketplace failures, had finally succumbed to the alternating highs of euphoria and lows of despondency. He had begun regular sessions with a shrink. And in his particular case, in line with the theory that converts are usually the most convinced of their new beliefs, I thought that his longstanding and steadfast dismissal of psychiatry as quackery boded well for the possibility that he could find some comfort on his counselor's couch.

And indeed, he went at it with a vengeance, devoting numerous lunch hours every week to his sessions. A few months later, when I asked how it was going with the good doctor, he looked at me sadly and just shook his head.

"What's the problem?" I asked.

"The problem seems to be *my* problems," he answered.

"I don't get it," I said.

"At the end of my last session, he told me he didn't want to see me any more," he replied.

"Isn't that usually the patient's line?"

"Yeah, well, I guess you can call it a Freudian 'first,' " he quipped.

"What are you gonna do?"

" I dunno," he answered, "it's bad enough to get fired by a client. But when you get fired by somebody *you* hired, I'd say that's rock bottom. The good news is, I've got nowhere to go but up."

"Do you have another doctor?" I asked.

"Nah, screw the shrinks," he said. "I can live without 'em."

And he did. He worked, and succeeded, and even learned to relax once in a while in the years thereafter. He just drove the rest of us nuts.

The Morning After

I met Len Vickers soon after joining BBDO and we've remained good friends ever since. We worked together on a couple of accounts, he as the account executive and I as the copywriter. We came from quite different cultural but similar economic backgrounds, Len having grown up in the working class of northern England, while I was brought up a New Yorker, not from any fashionable part of Manhattan but from a middle-class neighborhood in Queens.

We shared an often cynical view, not so much about the role of advertising in the market-driven scheme of things but largely about the relationships between agencies and clients, which we assumed were not peculiar to BBDO but were rather conditions endemic to the business. We believed very much in the power of communications to affect people's attitudes and behavior, which is, of course, the basic objective of advertising. But it always struck us as ridiculously self-defeating that too many clients generally afford their agencies little of the deference or respect that professional expertise should warrant. They pay us for the advertising we produce but more often than not, pay little or no attention to our recommendations, opinions, and advice.

Or put another way, they know they can't do what we do

but they tend to believe they know more about it than we do. Many do not hesitate to dismiss an advertising campaign specifically devised to meet their strategic needs by simply judging it to be wrong based on their inexperienced instinct rather than any informed experience. I liken it to telling a doctor or lawyer you don't agree with their diagnosis or counsel and therefore want them to think of something different. Admittedly, our work does not require the study, training, and licensing of the medical and legal professions. But there are at least as many fools with M.D.s and Esquires after their names as there are in advertising, yet we don't hesitate to sometimes stake our lives or liberty on their opinions.

Maybe it has to do with the fact that because everybody is exposed to advertising practically all the time, everybody thinks they know a great deal about it. But that's tantamount to believing that if you watch enough *ER* or *Law and Order,* you are qualified to make medical or legal judgments.

You can either get mad about the indifferent attitude of such clients or laugh at it. Len and I chose mostly to laugh. But he never lapsed into being "holier than thou" about it. In fact, he did the unthinkable. He became a client.

Len left BBDO to join Jack Welch at GE at the time Jack was rethinking GE's advertising. Len's intellect, innovativeness, and impatience with the status quo made him a perfect choice for Jack's reordering of GE priorities. Len saw the extensive reach of GE products and services, and the promise of Jack's new leadership as the way for him to influence the business model of one of America's most powerful and ubiquitous companies, creating growth in categories far more stimulating than the razors, deodorants, or household cleaners he worked on at the agency.

Thus, Len moved from "server" to "servee," which made for an ironic twist in our relationship. While we fully appreciated each other's strengths, now BBDO had a client who had participated in, and was therefore intimately familiar with, our inconsistencies and irrationalities. At the same time, we were fully aware of his propensity for obsessing about the communications process, sometimes, we thought, to the point of going beyond the practical capabilities of our craft.

And so it went. Len did indeed create change in GE's approach to market and business development, as well as their communications strategies and advertising programs. In turn, we created more dramatic, more effective, and more satisfying work for GE, largely because we really did appreciate each other and were never dismissive of our respective opinions. Together, over the course of many years, we developed and produced one of the best corporate branding campiagns we had ever created — "We Bring Good Things to Life."

But it wasn't easy. Agencies tend to be anarchic and undisciplined by nature, and when you have a client like Len, sometimes as detached from the everyday as his often mismatched shoes, socks, shirts, and ties would suggest, even the best intentions and personal relations can be put to the test. We usually react better to specifically focused assignments rather than thinking about our work as part of the broader, generally holistic objectives that often characterized Len's thinking

This became dramatically apparent one evening when Len, Bruce Crawford, then CEO of the agency, and I wound up debating and drinking into the early hours of the morning.

It began at dinner after a long meeting at the agency between GE and BBDO staffs. We had reserved a private room at 21, the clubby, business- and society-oriented restaurant known for catering to the well-heeled. Jack Welch was in a particularly provocative mood, mischievously setting up and stimulating an argument between Len and Bruce. As always, Len advocated a greater recognition of the power of advertising to actually lead a company's business strategy and mobilize its people as it sought to develop new opportunities for growth. Bruce responded with his typical impatience with what he considered academic theorizing about advertising playing anything more than its commercial role in selling products. Jack watched with impish glee as they went at it. Bottle of wine followed bottle of wine as the debate intensified.

Finally, Jack left but we didn't, moving to the famous and crowded bar at 21 to continue the now vociferous and disorderly discussion. We weren't there long, however, before the raucous dispute resulted in our being escorted out of the club. I last saw Len and Bruce on their way into the lobby of the building where Bruce owned an apartment. Len, who lived near the GE headquarters almost fifty miles from the city, would stay overnight at Bruce's place since it was far too late to head home.

The next morning my assistant asked me if I knew where Len was.

"Why are you asking?" I said.

"Because," she said, "there are about twenty people from GE in our boardroom waiting for him. I think he's supposed to be running a meeting with them here in the agency."

I called Bruce's apartment. His wife, Chris, answered the phone.

"Oh, I don't think Bruce will be coming in this morning," she said, recognizing my voice. "He was out very late last night."

"I know but I'm not calling about Bruce." I said, "Do me a favor and take a look around your apartment and see if Len Vickers is there."

"Why would he be here?" Chris asked.

"It's a long story, Chris," I answered. "but let's just say we were out late after the GE dinner and he didn't go home. I think he's sleeping somewhere in your place and I need to find him."

After a few minutes, she came back on the line.

"I don't believe what I'm seeing, but Len is lying on the floor of the living room with his leg draped over a coffee table in front of our sofa and his head almost in the fireplace."

"Can you tell if he's breathing?" I asked, not altogether facetiously.

"Well, he's making funny noises, so I assume he's alive," Chris replied. "But he won't be for long if Bruce sees his foot on that table. It's a very valuable antique."

"That will be the least of his problems if he's not over here soon," I told Chris. "There's a roomful of GE managers waiting for him, so it would be good if you can find a way to get him off the table, out of the fireplace, and over to the agency as fast as possible."

Twenty minutes later, I saw Len come out of the elevator and head for our boardroom. His suit was a wrinkled mess, his tie hung unknotted from his untucked shirt, and I was afraid he was going to go head over heels, tripping on his untied shoelaces.

Uh, oh, I thought as I watched him enter the room, *they're really going to be pissed off at him in there.*

"My deepest apologies for keeping you waiting," I heard Len declare in a voice that made me think of Churchill entering the House of Commons. "It seems that Jack and I have had a bit of a disagreement this morning, and as you can see, he wanted to be sure I got his point."

The room dissolved in laughter and the crisis ended. Len's tenure at GE went on for years, with Len going through both the thrill of victories and the agony of defeats as he pursued his programs. Jack's initial success in leading GE resulted largely from his reducing the basic cost structure and bureaucracy of the organization, and concentrating on reordering its diverse portfolio of businesses, closing some and buying others. Len foresaw a future whole that could become greater than the sum of its parts, by finding and promoting unity that would avoid the "conglomerate" label usually applied to GE's diversity. Len knew that Jack's objectives were essential, but at the end of the day, he realized that Jack's famously productive pragmatism was not necessarily directed toward exploiting the longer-term opportunities that were Len's vision and passion.

He went on to a similar marketing position at Xerox, eventually retiring to consult with various companies on their business development, branding, and corporate communications programs. But beneath Len's boisterous laugh and good companionship, there will always be an edge of disappointment in his demeanor. He's a very bright and visionary man who has had a successful career in business, but he admits to a lingering regret at not having pursued his love for writing and politics.

Anyway, he will certainly not be envious of this book since his view of it will no doubt be something along the lines of "What piffle!" And I cannot believe that anyone with Len's sharp sense of the ludicrous could look at politics today and still want to get into that business.

So what's left for us is to keep laughing. Which we will.

Fasten Your Seat Belts

Every so often, BBDO considered the idea of providing private jet transportation for its top executives. Despite being primarily a New York agency, most of our domestic clients had their headquarters in far-flung and sometimes hard-to-reach cities.

At one time or another, our client list included Apple, Visa, and Chevron, all in or near San Francisco; Chrysler in Detroit; Pillsbury in Minneapolis, and Hormel, a long car ride from there; Frito-Lay outside Dallas; Pizza Hut in Witchita, R. J. Reynolds in Winston-Salem; DuPont in Wilmington; Wrigley and Quaker Oats in Chicago; Gillette in Boston; Burger King in Miami; Armstrong in Lancaster, Pennsylvania; Delta in Atlanta; and so on. And we operated major agencies in Canada and Mexico. In addition, new business presentations often brought us to any number of other, and some not very accessible, North American locations.

In some instances, it wasn't only long distances or remote destinations that caused travel problems. For our trips to North Carolina, for example, even though it was only a ninety-minute flight, airline scheduling made it impossible for us to be there for a morning meeting without traveling the night before.

Clearly, we could save considerable time by owning or leasing our own plane, not to mention avoiding the hassles of commercial flights, which were considerable even before the restrictions imposed by the attacks of 9/11. The one thing we could not save, however, was money. On the contrary, no matter how complicated or frequent the trips, every analysis we did proved conclusively that it would cost the company significantly more to use a private jet than to travel on scheduled flights, even at first-class fares. And despite the fact that many of our clients had fleets of planes, they would surely look askance at their advertising agency jetting in and out of town in planes of our own.

As my predecessor in running the company, Bruce Crawford, once observed to the BBDO board of directors, "The only rationale to clients and shareholders for incurring the increased expense of investing in our own plane would be to extend the life of the chief executive. And I doubt," he concluded ruefully, "that very many of them would care about that."

Nevertheless, that did not deter us from occasionally revisiting the issue. It was an ongoing example of wishful thinking best expressed by Phil Dusenberry, our creative leader for more than two decades, who worked as an advertising volunteer on President Ronald Reagan's re-election team in 1984. After returning from a trip with the president to film his visit to Normandy commemorating the fortieth anniversary of the D-Day invasion, Phil talked to me about the trip.

"Allen, I've gotta tell you," he said, with a faraway and wistful look, "flying on Air Force One is the only way to travel."

So we were certainly not going to discourage any prospective jet leasing or chartering company from pitching us to become their client, particularly since it almost always included a free ride on one of their most opulently appointed aircraft. On one such occasion, as a couple of us enjoyed the luxury of swiveling and reclining in our heavily cushioned leather seats, our every food and drink whim instantly satisfied by a flight attendant serving actually edible fare, one of the pilots joined us to present the case for his company's services, which of course, we were obliged to hear.

First, he rambled on about the many reasons we should fly privately instead of commercially, all of which were already on our wish list. Then, as expected, he made the case for his company's professional experience, qualifications, and the variety of aircraft that would be available to us on practically a moment's notice. And predictably, he concluded with the one factor we knew would be an exaggeration beyond what even we in advertising would consider acceptable hyperbole — the cost effectiveness of the service.

To avoid showing a lack of interest in the face of his enthusiasm, I told him I had a personal question. "I'm curious to know," I said, "whether you and the other pilots in your company are qualified to fly commercial jets for the major airlines."

"Absolutely," he responded without a moment's hesitation. "All of us are fully licensed by the FAA to fly for American, United, Delta, or anyone."

"Well, I understand those guys make a pretty good buck for a lot fewer hours than you put in," I went on. "What is it, eighty hours a month maximum? That would be a twenty-hour week, right?"

"Yeah, we work at least double that," he said.

"And they probably make more money than you, right?"

"Yeah, you can bet on that," he answered.

"So tell me," I asked, "why do you fly private jets instead of commercial airliners?"

He paused for a minute as a wide grin slowly crept across his face. "The truth is," he said, "me and my buddies, we do it for the *excitement*."

"Excuse me?" I exclaimed, eyebrows raised in wide-eyed astonishment.

"Hey, there's nothin' more boring than flying a commercial jet," he said. "Y' know," he continued with growing enthusiasm, "those guys have equipment on board that can fly the plane without them from almost anywhere to anywhere, and that includes take-offs and landings. They could go from New York to L.A. without ever touching the controls. Man, I wanna *fly* a plane," he said leaning forward for emphasis. "I don't wanna just sit in it."

"Okay, I get it," I said with a smile. "You're kidding me about this 'excitement' thing, right?"

"No way!" he exclaimed, completely serious. "And besides, we hit some pretty awesome places, not the same cities over and over again. Y' know what I mean? The playgrounds of the rich and famous — resort towns, vacation spots, great night clubs, terrific women. Hell, who'd wanna fly commercial compared to that?"

"Me!" I blurted out, shuddering at the thought of a hungover Red Baron at the controls of my plane, doing loop-the-loops to keep himself entertained. "I like the idea of a pilot who's happy being bored out of mind and spending his nights asleep in bed."

But I still gladly fly in private jets whenever I'm invited, or there's no other way to get where I have to be, when I have to be there. It's as close to Air Force One as I'm likely to get.

And I'm sure that just as in the Lears and Gulfstreams, there are also a few idiots in the cockpits of commercial airliners, not to mention other practitioners of other professions that serve us.

When all is said and flown, it's better not to think about it. You don't really want to know what's going through a surgeon's head when he cuts you open.

My Son, the Liar

During his administration, President George H. W. Bush and Mrs. Bush both strongly supported the Partnership for a Drug-Free America. As president, Mr. Bush appeared in some of our commercials and also offered the White House as a venue for various press briefings and industry receptions to further our efforts. For her part, Mrs. Bush appeared at PDFA events, lending stature to, and stimulating interest in, our programs.

On one occasion, the president had agreed to take part in a cocktail party at the White House to thank leaders of the major television and print media companies for their donations of time and space to run the advertising that the Partnership had created.

Even before the heightened security precautions resulting from the 9/11 attacks on New York and Washington, getting people cleared to enter the White House was no routine matter. All attendees had to be pre-screened, providing the Secret Service with names, addresses, places and dates of birth, social security numbers, and the like. Despite the desire of the Partnership to therefore limit the attendance only to those for whom the reception was actually intended, I wangled an invitation for my college freshman son, Jonathan, to join me.

I thought being in the White House and meeting the president would be impressive and memorable for him, and having experienced it under my auspices would mitigate any doubts that popular lampooning and academic contempt might have instilled in him about the credibility of his father's profession.

At gatherings such as this, the people meeting the president usually wear name tags so he can refer to them personally at a glance instead of taking up his time with lengthier formal introductions. Even though Jon was still in school, it was far easier to justify his presence by having his name tag, like mine, identify him as coming from BBDO. As we milled about, awaiting the president, I offered him a little advice.

"When we meet the president," I said, "he's going to look at our name tags and see that we have the same name from the same company. I'll mention you're my son but I'd guess that to say something personal, he'll probably make some comment about us working together."

"Well, I'll tell him I go to school," said Jon, "but since you run BBDO and you're my father, I'll just explain that it was simpler to do it this way."

"No, that's not my point, Jon," I said. "Believe me, he won't really care if we both work at the agency or not. He'll just be saying it to show some interest in us. The best thing for you to do is let him assume you work with me, tell him it's an honor to meet him, and let it go at that."

At that moment, someone rushed into the room and attached the presidential seal to the front of a lectern. I had thought this emblem would always be a permanently engraved fixture throughout the White House and found it comical that the seal the world probably saw most often was actually a portable piece of cardboard with tape on the back, which someone carried wherever the president went. Moments later, a voice announced, "Ladies and gentlemen, the president of the United States," and Mr. Bush joined us to a round of applause. After a few words of welcome and appreciation to the media executives whom the Partnership had invited, the president began moving around the room, shaking hands, and exchanging a few words with each of the guests as he met them. When he came to Jon and me, he immediately looked at our name tags.

"Thank you for doing this, Mr. President," I said. "I'm a volunteer with the Partnership and this is my son, Jon."

"Your group is doing our country a great service," Mr. Bush responded. Then, as predicted, he asked, "Say, Jon, do you work with your dad?"

The ensuing pause no doubt did not last nearly as long as it seemed at the moment. "Yes, sir," he said at last.

"Well, you fellas keep up the good work," said the president as he moved on to his next handshake.

During the rest of the time we remained at the reception, I could tell that Jon was upset. He's a very intense person and it's usually easy to see when he feels something is wrong. When we finally left the White House and got into a cab to return to the airport, I asked him what was bothering him.

"I can't believe you did that to me," he blurted out.

"What are you talking about?" I asked, honestly perplexed.

"I just can't believe it. I can't believe you made me *lie* to the president of the United States."

"Well, Jon," I laughed, "it wasn't the first time that somebody lied to him today. And it won't be the last time either."

Jon would tell you that's terrible. I would say that's life. But it would be a better world if more people agreed with him.

The Big Upset

Armstrong has been a client of BBDO since long before I was born and as a result, has a very special place in our company's history. They are far from being our largest client in terms of their sales or how much they spend on advertising. But in a business where clients come and go, and where relationships can change suddenly and drastically based on the whims and egos of a new management taking over the marketing and advertising reins, having a client who stays with the agency decade after decade is something to take pride in and celebrate.

So no matter who was CEO of our company, Armstrong had his attention. When I became creative director of BBDO in New York, I made it my business to visit them at the earliest opportunity.

It was not the easiest trip. Their headquarters are in Lancaster, a small town in the middle of the Amish country in eastern Pennsylvania, and no matter which mode of transportation you choose, it takes more than four hours to cover the few hundred miles between our offices. We usually drove since rail service required changing trains in Philadelphia, and there were no commercial flights available. Of course, a private jet could get there from New York in about a half hour, but the cost per mile would make it one of the most expensive trips in America.

In any event, this was an obligation, not an option. So off I dutifully went.

In fact, being there was far more pleasant and peaceful than visiting the big cities that house most corporate headquarters. The Amish live in a beautiful countryside with picturesque farmland and communities surrounding the typically middle-class American town of Lancaster. And almost all the people we dealt with at Armstrong reflected a far less frantic lifestyle and attitude than the usual hyperactive pace and posturing of big business.

For practically a generation, Don Goldstrom led the marketing and advertising programs of the company, which made him the person with whom we most often spent our time. My introduction to Armstrong began with meeting Don the evening before a day of reviews and presentations he had scheduled for my benefit.

Don personified much of the Armstrong culture. Despite his imposing height of about six feet five inches, he was as quiet, and when he talked, as soft-spoken as a librarian in a reading room. His intelligence was always apparent, while whatever ego he may have had was not. He never talked just to hear his own voice, and the remarks he made were carefully considered. Even the almost languid movements of his lanky frame seemed thought out in advance. Don took his responsibilities quite seriously and he worked diligently to keep in touch with any trends and developments in marketing and media that might affect Armstrong's advertising. He was the perfect fit of an executive officer in a company whose commanders traditionally did not carry the figurative swagger sticks typical of many self-styled captains of industry.

However, this was the man I only came to know and appreciate over the years. When we shook hands for the first time and sat down to dinner, I had no idea what to expect. Don quickly put me at ease with a few polite questions about my upbringing, my family, and my career at the agency.

Given his height and my own interest in basketball, having played in school, I eventually asked him if he followed the sport.

"Not really," he answered, "I'm more interested in football."

"Did you play in college?" I asked.

"Yes," he said, "I played varsity for four years."

"Did you ever think about playing pro ball?" I continued, having found a subject that could allow me to show the same interest in him as he had in me.

"Oh, no," he said. "I was never nearly good enough. Although," he continued, "in my senior year at Penn, I did play with Chuck Bednarik. Do you remember him? He was an all-pro middle linebacker with the Philadelphia Eagles."

"I'm a Giant fan," I said. "How could I forget the guy who nearly killed Frank Gifford?"

"Well, it may have been the Ivy League," said Don, "but Bednarik was an animal even then. Gifford wasn't the first guy he sent to the hospital. He nearly took my head off just in a practice scrimmage. Where did you go to school?" he asked, shifting the conversation back to me.

"Columbia," I answered. "I guess we're both Ivy Leaguers."

"How'd you come to go there?" he asked.

"Being from New York, it was the best school I could go to without having to pay for room and board. And my brother went there before me, so it was kind of in the family," I explained. "But the funny thing is, the first time I ever heard of Columbia was listening to a football game on the radio. I remember it distinctly because it was when they played Army and broke their thirty-five game winning streak. That was when Army had Blanchard and Davis, and they were supposed to be unbeatable," I continued, determined to show Don my knowledge and enthusiasm for his favorite sport. "My brother was jumping up and down on his bed, cheering like a maniac when Columbia won 20–19 in the last minute on some impossible touchdown catch by Bob Swiacki."

"Actually, the score was 21–20 and the guy's name was *Bill* Swiacki," said Don very softly, I thought so as not to show he was correcting me.

"Boy, my brother really hated Army," I went on, "I guess because he was almost near the age for getting drafted. I remember him saying how great it was that 'those Neanderthal assholes' lost to a team like Columbia who he said 'couldn't beat a local high school.' "

"Well, he was right about Columbia being a pretty bad football team," said Don. "We should have beaten them by fifty points."

"Excuse me, Don, but did you say *'we'*?" I asked.

"Oh, yes," he said. "I was one of those 'Neanderthal assholes' in that game against Columbia. I played end for Army for two years before transferring to Penn."

Totally embarrassed, I didn't know what to say. I just sat there thinking, *Now who's the asshole?*

After a few moments, Don broke the silence. "Armstrong seven, BBDO nothing," he said, laughing. And in all the years I knew him, he never replayed that game, much to my relief.

It Ain't Worth the Hassle

Soon after the founding of Omnicom Group, which became the holding company of three agencies — BBDO, Doyle Dane Bernbach, and Needham Harper — the CEO of the newly formed DDB Needham, Keith Reinhard, joined me, as head of Omnicom, for a visit with Wayne Calloway, chief executive of PepsiCo.

One of the strategic reasons for creating Omnicom was the notion that with more resources under one roof, we could offer large clients the quid pro quo of reducing the total cost of their marketing and advertising programs if they would assign more of their brands to our agencies — in effect, a volume discount. Since both BBDO and DDB Needham handled some PepsiCo brands in the beverage and snack food categories, it would be a natural extension of our responsibilities, which we believed the agencies and the client managers could adapt to with relative ease.

Wayne was a Southern gentleman, who had left being a "good ol' boy" behind, but who still maintained some of his Dixie drawl and syntax. He was very astute, more of a businessman with considerable financial expertise than a marketing or advertising executive. He had a passion for motorcycles, which helped distinguish him as literally and figuratively a down-to-earth guy.

Unlike many other captains of industry, Wayne did not wear his stripes on his sleeves for all to see and salute. Nor did his smart, self-assured way of making decisions develop into an ego that would tolerate no discussion or dissent. Keith and I shared a high degree of confidence that Wayne would listen to us, see the benefit to his company of our idea, and quickly take us up on it.

With his customary warmth, Wayne turned our visit into a lunch on the patio of his country club near PepsiCo's head-quarters in the suburbs of New York City. After some friendly banter about our families and mutual acquaintances, inquiries as to the general state of our business, and placing our orders, Wayne got us to the point.

"Well, fellas, what's on your minds today?" he asked with a smile.

"Wayne," I began, "Keith and I have an idea that could be a profitable situation for both PepsiCo and Omnicom. It should result in lower marketing and advertising costs for you and more business for us."

"Okay, buddy, I sure like the sound of the first part of your proposition," said Wayne with a wink. "What's the deal?"

"As you know," I continued, "since we put our agencies together in Omnicom, we're handling a significant amount of PepsiCo business in both your major product categories. Obviously," I went on, "we can't work for anyone else in either the snack food or the soft drink business, so the only way we can grow in those areas is with you. If you'll get your divisions to give us more brands to handle, we can afford to charge less than you're now paying us and others for the same work."

"And," Keith added, "because we've pooled and strength-ened many of the non-advertising services like sales promo-tion and public relations our agencies used to offer separately, we can be more efficient in taking on more assignments in those areas and create further savings for PepsiCo."

"That it?" said Wayne. "Okay, now lemme see if I've got this straight." Neither Keith nor I believed for an instant that he didn't know exactly what we were suggesting and had already determined his response, which we felt sure would be to go ahead with our plan.

"You guys can take on a lot more of our ad business," Wayne continued, cocking his eye and looking skyward as though speculating to himself, "and we're gonna pay a lot less to get it done than we're payin' now. An' all I gotta do is tell my guys to go along, right?"

"Right," I responded enthusiastically, fully confident that his next words would seal the deal.

"Can't do it, buddy," said Wayne.

After a moment of stunned silence, I recovered only enough to say, "I'm really surprised, Wayne."

"Well, lemme tell you a little story," said Wayne, with just an additional hint of "down-home" folksiness. "See, I could save this company a pot-load of money every year just by writin' a little memo that says from now on, every truck we lease in every division of the enterprise is gonna come from one truckin' company, under one contract, and I'm gonna be the guy who makes that deal for everybody. 'Cause I know for a fact," Wayne said, now poking a finger at Keith and me for emphasis, "that our purchasin' folks in every division have their own contracts with their own suppliers and every one of them has convinced their bosses that they've done a real good job by makin' a real good deal. An' they probably have, when you look at it just from their point of view. But when you add it all up, you know an' I know it's a lot more than we'd be payin' one supplier."

"So why don't you write that memo?" I asked, more from frustration than good sense. I realized the moment I asked it how dumb my question was, since that was obviously going to be the point of Wayne's story.

"Yeah, I'm gettin' to that, buddy," said Wayne, too polite to point out the stupidity of my comment. "I'm not gonna do it for the same reason I'm not gonna tell my people which ad agencies they oughtta do business with. See, they're gonna resent my gettin' into their operations when I'm holdin' them responsible for their profitability. Even if it makes them more money, they'll get all hot an' bothered 'cause it would've been *my* decision, not theirs. They're not gonna appreciate it much that I'm showin' them up. An' the next time they gotta make a decision, they're gonna spend their time tryin' to figure out what I'm gonna think, instead of doin' their jobs. D' you see my point?" Wayne concluded, knowing full well that we did and that the discussion was over.

"Bottom line, buddy," he added, "it ain't worth the hassle."

After lunch and a few final pleasantries, Keith and I headed back to our offices, having learned a lesson we would put to frequent use, as both of us struggled to bring separate companies together in a business driven by people whose knee-jerk reaction is too often to protect their ego and turf.

Sometimes being right just ain't worth the hassle.

Note: Some years later, PepsiCo and Omnicom did in fact make such an agreement, which many changes in both businesses made more imperative.

The BBDO Philharmonic Orchestra

Every year or so, BBDO brings together the managers of all our companies from around the world for a few days of meetings and socializing. Many corporations do this as a way to communicate their business objectives, to foster greater understanding and cooperation among the diverse geographies and cultures that comprise a global organization, to enhance their corporate pride, and to energize the competitive spirit their leaders will bring to the enterprise.

One of the tactics that companies use to build enthusiasm at their gatherings is to employ someone known as a "motivational speaker." Their objective is the same as the coach of a sports team who delivers a rousing locker room speech before the big game so that the training and skill of the players will be enhanced by a rush of adrenalin and emotion.

Recently, after some very difficult years in the advertising business, we felt that this type of presentation could help overcome negative feelings stemming from contentious issues that had arisen among some of our managers due to the pressures of the economic downturn we had all experienced. In fact, as a cost-saving measure, we had not met for three years, so this was an important opportunity to regenerate an upbeat attitude and rebuild our efforts to work together for our mutual benefit.

Our only problem was the choice of speaker.

Because we are an international company with managers from all regions of the world, the name or credentials of our presenter would have to be universally recognized. The obvious analogies between the highly competitive natures of sports and business have turned many star athletes and coaches into corporate motivators. But personalities from the world's most popular sport, soccer, are virtually unknown in America, while our Super Bowl and World Series heroes go practically unnoticed beyond our borders. In addition, justified or not, we like to think of ourselves as a comparatively cultured and sophisticated crowd that would reject a mere jock — even basketball's globally glamorized Michael Jordan — as a source of personal or professional inspiration.

Given the need for prominence and acceptability, I became more and more depressed as we considered and rejected speaker after speaker, either because we felt they failed to meet our criteria, or they placed a far greater value on their appearance than we were prepared to offer. (How many people would you pay seven figures, provide a round trip via private jet, and put them up in a top hotel's biggest suite just to hear them talk for half an hour?)

Luckily, I happened to mention our problem to one of our global clients who had recently conducted a similar meeting. He immediately recommended a speaker he claimed had been a tremendous success in generating an atmosphere of excitement and goodwill among their executives from all over the world — Benjamin Zander, conductor of the Boston Philharmonic Orchestra.

"Really? A musician?" I said. "I can understand he might talk about an orchestra being like a diverse group of managers who have to work together and so on, but I can't see how that kind of cliché would motivate your group or ours."

"Well, it wasn't like that at all," he responded. "He didn't talk much about music or orchestras or being a conductor. But he did have us all on our feet singing together at the top of our lungs. And we *loved* it."

"What the hell were you singing?" I asked in amazement.

"We started off with 'Happy Birthday' and ended up with Beethoven's 'Ode to Joy,' in German, I might add."

"You're kidding me," I said.

"Do it," said my client. "You won't be sorry."

I thanked him for his advice and got in touch with the maestro. I was a little worried that our group of about three hundred sometimes self-satisfied business entrepreneurs and often self-styled creative egotists might find singing together a rather childish beginning to a company conference. But the un-qualified endorsement from our client convinced me.

Thus did Maestro Zander come to address our assembled company. His performance was amazing. He had us singing the most mundane and mindless birthday greeting with fervor and feeling usually reserved for a military fight song, which was exactly his point. He regaled us for two hours with great poignancy and wit about the value of positive personal com-mitment in all our endeavors, as opposed to the knee-jerk cyn-icism or rote performance to which we were all too prone. He inspired us to shun the fear and trembling of corporate compe-tition by celebrating the learning that comes from mistakes, in-stead of wasting our energy avoiding them. And he concluded by bringing us to our feet in a roaring rendition of the joy Beethoven must have intended when he composed his famous ode.

The effect on our group was beyond anything I could have hoped for. We were totally captivated by one of the most effective, most memorable, and indeed most motivating pre-sentations on any of our meeting agendas.

I sometimes wonder what kind of performance I might have given if Zander had asked me to speak to the Boston Philharmonic Orchestra. Fortunately, he didn't.

Extra Innings

Some years ago, when the baseball team I've rooted for all my life, the New York Yankees, was suffering a decade of decline, I had the opportunity to see a game with my boss at BBDO, also a lifelong Yankee fan. And it had been arranged for us to meet two of the team's biggest stars — Catfish Hunter and Thurman Munson — after the game.

With only about a week left in the season, and the Yankees again out of playoff contention, the only thing noteworthy about that particular game was that Hunter would be pitching for his twentieth win of the season, traditionally a milestone performance. He had already established himself as a star pitcher with the Oakland Athletics, whom he left for considerably more money offered by George Steinbrenner, then a new owner of the Yankees. Munson was also a bona fide star, recognized as one of baseball's best catchers, and the captain of the team.

Despite the disappointment of the Yankee's poor record, it was a great thrill for us to sit in the first row directly behind home plate where we could see and almost feel the power of Hunter's pitching. After the Yankees had won the game, with Hunter earning credit for the victory, my boss and I looked forward to what was admittedly, for both of us, the even greater thrill of going into the Yankee clubhouse to see Hunter and Munson. Had we known that we would spend the next couple of hours in a bar, drinking and talking baseball with the two of them, we would have been even more excited.

As it was, we proudly showed our passes and entered the inner sanctum of baseball's most storied team. If I thought I was taken with being in the presence of these household names, it was nothing compared to my boss's obvious state of rapture. He stood almost transfixed by the sight of one Yankee after another, some heading to and from the showers, some sitting at their lockers in various states of dress between their uniforms and street clothes. My boss was religiously homophobic, but watching him, I thought some latent tendency might be emerging in the presence of so much male athletic greatness. To put it bluntly, he was practically sniffing their jockstraps. His bliss turned to near ecstasy when Hunter and Munson suggested we walk over to a local bar for some drinks.

Once we had settled into a booth and ordered our first round, the conversation drifted between baseball and questions about our respective families and upbringing. My boss, who was accustomed to multiple drinks at lunch and after work, kept the cocktails coming, but with the ball players sticking to beer, and me doing my well-practiced trick of ordering straight shots that I could easily pour under the table, he was soon the only one feeling the effects of the alcohol.

"Boy, I gotta tell you guys," he said with the beginnings of a slur to his words, "I'd give my right arm to be in your shoes."

"Well, I hope you're a lefty," said Munson, laughing.

"Hey, c'mon Thurman," he said, "you know what I mean. What a great life you have, playing ball every day and getting paid millions to do it."

"It ain't all that easy, mah friend," said Hunter in his slow, southern drawl. "Most of the time, ah'd rather be in mah pickup, headin' out to do some shootin'."

"Aw, that's baloney, Catfish," said my boss, having left any sense of inhibition in one of his cocktail glasses. "You can't tell me that playing for the New York Yankees isn't the greatest thrill any man can have in his whole lifetime."

"Well, if he can't, I can," retorted Munson. "I been a Yankee my whole career and lemme tell ya man, it can get old after a while. I can't say I'd rather be doin' anything else, but havin' George all over your ass every time you lose a game, an' havin' your kids read what bums you are when you don't live up to the great Yankee tradition, an' goin' home to watch some other team in the playoffs every year, it can get to be a real drag, money or no money." Then, as an afterthought, he asked, "You know why I grew this bushy moustache? I'll tell ya, it's just to piss off George, 'cause he hates it an' there ain't a fuckin' thing he can do about it."

"Yuh got that right, ol' buddy," chimed in Hunter.

"Well, I've gotta believe that Mr. Steinbrenner is a great owner and a real leader," said my boss, somewhat sullenly. "I wouldn't think twice about working for him no matter how tough he is," he said, almost defiantly.

"Well I would," I blurted out, thinking about the similarities between my boss's dedication to ruling by fear and Steinbrenner's well-known bullying.

"Well now," said Hunter to my boss, "looks like you did all the talkin' but *he* did all the listenin'."

"I sure hope he didn't hear that," I said to Hunter, "'cause I can't throw a curve and I can't hit worth a shit. I need the job I have."

"Don't worry, pal," said Munson, laughing. "I don't think he's heard anything in the past half hour. Anyway, it's bedtime for the ballplayers, so thanks for the beers." Then, as we were leaving the bar, he said to me with a wink, "And tomorrow, tell your boss we think he's a great guy."

"Yeah, man," added Hunter, laughing, "almost as great as Steinbrenner."

The next morning, my boss called me on the phone.

"What a great night, what terrific guys!" he exclaimed. "I'd give my right arm to be one of them."

I breathed a sigh of relief. "Then I hope you're a lefty," I said.

The Birds

One of the earliest major presentations of advertising I made was at Gillette headquarters in Boston. Our assignment was to suggest new varieties of their Foamy shaving cream and to create television commercials for each of them.

At the time, a new technology called "micro-encapsulation" made it possible to embed aromatic particles in the product that would later be released when the shaving cream was propelled from the can and came in contact with the air. Thus it was possible for Foamy to market an extended line of shaving creams with different scents, which was the idea behind the new campaigns I was to present.

First we had to come up with the particular aromas that we thought would be appealing to men as they shaved in the morning, and then give each of this new array of products an appealing name. Our candidates included ideas such as: Morning Mist, Lemon Tree, Wavin' Wheat, Lime Twist, Lavender, and Peaches 'n' Cream. Of course, during our brainstorming sessions, our perpetual propensity for bathroom humor produced a number of less appropriate but entertaining thoughts like: Factory Fog, Dumpster Dew, Pasture Patty, and the inevitably scatological Passing Wind, obviously none of which ever saw the light of a client meeting.

Once we had selected the specific new products that we would recommend, we had to develop storyboards to depict each commercial. (This technique is a series of drawings that showed the action we intended to film with the accompanying sound track — the music, dialog and/or announcer script — typed below each picture.) But to bring the storyboard to life for the clients, and to let them understand how it would play on TV, we had to dramatize it by describing the scenes, performing the roles, and giving them a sense of how the audio would sound.

This was what I nervously headed for Boston to do, armed with ideas for about a dozen new Foamy formulations and a choice of storyboards for each, showing the commercials that could introduce it to consumers.

But it was more than just the size of the presentation and the critical need for the Foamy brand to increase its sales by expanding its offering that made my Boston debut especially intimidating. It was the fact that the president of Gillette's Toiletries Division would attend, something he rarely did at this early stage of development. His presence signaled the importance of the project. And naturally, he was accompanied by everyone at Gillette who had anything to do with the Foamy brand.

Because the client was out in force, the agency was obliged to show an equal interest by top management, resulting in BBDO's chairman, president, creative director, and a full coterie of account executives in attendance as well. So in practically my first time at bat in advertising's major leagues, I was facing not only one of our highest ranking clients, but also my boss, his boss, and my boss's boss's boss.

I don't mind admitting I was in a less than sanguine state of mind. I had always thought the idea of being so terrified that your knees knocked was only apocryphal, but as I stood up to begin, I quickly learned otherwise. My knees weren't just knocking — they were actually *banging* together.

The first commercial in the campaign was for a new Foamy scent, Spring Breeze, in which the opening scene showed the sun rising over a suburban house as a light went on in one of the rooms. As the camera moved inside to watch a man who had just turned on his bathroom light preparing to shave, we would see the curtains rustling in the breeze coming through the open window and hear the sound of birds chirping. As I described the action, to more fully capture the sense of this bucolic moment, I intended to mimic the clipped, semi-melodic whistling of our little feathered friends.

There was only one problem. Not only were my knees in delirium tremens, my mouth was so dry that when I pursed my lips and blew, the only sound that came out was not a whistle or even a chirp — it was a barely audible whoosh of air, which I repeated three or four times in desperation but without any success. So there I stood, one minute into the show, with the top brass of Gillette and BBDO gaping at me in obvious astonishment as I tried to think of something — anything — to say or do that could get me past the flock of pathetically puffing birds I was portraying.

All of a sudden, I heard *a bird chirping*. I knew for sure it wasn't me, and when I looked toward the sound, I saw my boss in full twitter. A second later, he was joined by the president, followed by the chairman of BBDO, all three men in business suits, seated in a row at the massive oak table of the stately Gillette boardroom, tweeting away like birds at a worm-catching convention.

The client group all burst into laughter. Having been bailed out of what I was sure would be a disaster, I relaxed enough to carry on, giving at least an acceptable account of myself and the work we were showing.

In spite of my less than hit performance, the result was the eventual decision to market a new product, Foamy with Lemon-Lime, which research showed was the scent men would like best among all our entries. Our commercials, based on a mythical half-yellow, half-green hybrid fruit combining lemon and lime, were well liked by the client and consumers alike, helping produce a sales success.

And to my great relief, when I presented our storyboards for the new campaign, my confidence was bolstered by the fact that there are no known sounds that come from either lemons or limes.

Betting on Baseball

On the surface, baseball appears to be a simple game whose rules are not hard to understand, and whose strategies, compared to other major sports, are fairly easy to explain. Of course, it's true that on the professional level, hitting a baseball is arguably among the most difficult feats in all of sports. But that notwithstanding, the general aspects of playing the game would be fairly apparent even to a first-time spectator such as my mother, when I took her on a Saturday night to Yankee Stadium to see her first game.

Having grown up in Poland, she knew nothing about baseball except that my brother and I played it, listened to it on the radio, watched it when we finally got our first television set, and went to see the Yankees play whenever possible. But at the ball park, she caught on very quickly, asking relevant questions and seeming to enjoy the game even when it went into extra innings with not much happening offensively for either team. Finally, as midnight approached, the visiting team scored, but because of some arcane municipal law, the game could not continue once it became Sunday morning. So I explained that if the Yankees did not have their chance to bat before midnight, the visiting team's score would not count and the game would end as a tie.

The Yankee manager, Casey Stengel, was taking advantage of this rule by repeatedly climbing slowly up the dugout steps, shuffling at a snail's pace across the infield to talk with his pitcher, walking back to the dugout, and emerging again to replace him, a tactic designed to make it impossible for the Yankees to bat before the stroke of midnight. I expected my mother to be confused by this, so I prepared to explain.

"Look at what that *alter cocker* (Yiddish for "old fart") is doing," she exclaimed before I could say a word. "He's stalling."

As I said, it's not hard to figure out what's happening in a baseball game. But there are nevertheless many subtleties that are rarely noticed or commented on, even by those who know the game very well.

For example, I had a long-standing baseball bet with one of our account executives, Tom Villante, who had spent many years traveling with the old Brooklyn Dodgers, representing our clients who sponsored their broadcasts. For some reason that has long since escaped me, we got into a discussion over running the bases — specifically which foot a runner should use to touch a base as he ran past it. I claimed it was the right foot so that there would be no need to bring one foot across the other, which would make it more difficult to maintain a smooth and continuous running path. He insisted that the runner should use his left foot specifically so that he *would* cross over and therefore make a sharper turn toward the next base. It was about as esoteric a baseball argument as you could have, so much so that we could find no clear and unequivocal instructions in any baseball manual to settle the bet. And so it went on for months, coming up in every conversation we had about our clients' businesses and the advertising we were doing for them.

One day, Tom phoned, saying that I should come to his office because he had found a way for us to definitively settle the bet. When I walked in, sitting on his couch was a man I recognized instantly —Tommy Lasorda, manager of the Dodgers, who had by then moved to Los Angeles.

Tom introduced me and wasted no time getting to the point. "Tell him, Tommy. Which foot should a runner use to touch the base?"

"Well, Allen," said Lasorda, "I hate to disappoint ya in our first meeting, but he's right. Ya hit the bag with your left foot so's you can cross over with your right an' get on a straight line to the next base."

"You're not just saying that to support your buddy here, are you, Tommy?" I ventured.

"Nah," he replied, laughing, "why would I lie to a guy I just met?"

Later, I asked Tom why, if he was going to invoke Lasorda as his witness, he didn't just get him on the phone back when we started the argument.

"I figured if it took long enough, I could get you to up the ante. And besides, would you have believed it was really Lasorda you were talking to?" asked Tom.

"Probably not," I answered. "The funny thing is, since we made the bet, I've seen plenty of guys use their right foot rounding a base."

"Not the good ones," said Tom.

"Jackie Robinson was a great base runner and I'll bet you he didn't do it all the time," I said, a little petulantly.

"You're on!" Tom exclaimed. "Are you gonna trust me to call him," he said reaching for the phone, "or do you wanna ask him in person?"

Welcome to the Holiday Inn

During the time when my first marriage had become a separation, which would eventually end in divorce, I arranged for Missy to surreptitiously accompany me on a trip to Florida, where I was to attend a Burger King meeting.

At that time, we were far from ready to be seen as a couple either by clients or colleagues, so I planned on us taking a later flight than the others from the agency and staying in a motel rather than the resort where the meetings would take place. I had told our people that I would be rooming with a relative, which, while certainly not exactly the case, had at least a modicum of truth to it. In fact, Missy's sister lived nearby and her husband, a well-known local businessman, had made a reservation for us to have a suite in a Holiday Inn.

The events that ultimately made this a most memorable trip began with our flight from New York. We missed it, a result of last-minute preparation at the agency to put together our part in the meeting, compounded by the usual bumper-to-bumper city traffic. Racing through the airport to the departure gate got us there just in time to see the jetway door close, and to be adamantly refused any possibility of getting on board despite my out-of-breath story of a dying grandmother and my grieving parents coming to meet our plane. Our only choice was to arrive sometime well after midnight on the last flight of the evening.

I thought I should call the motel to let them know about our now very late arrival to insure that they would hold our reservation. The desk clerk promised that the suite would be ready whenever we got there and that their van would still meet the later flight. So, even faced with a couple of hours to kill at JFK, things were looking up. We were headed off to sunshine and balmy weather, and with the exception of a few meetings I needed to attend, we would have some time together away from the combined chaos of business and my unsettled personal life.

Little did I know.

We arrived, but the van from the motel did not. In the nearly empty airport, it was not likely that we had missed each other, so I called the motel, repeating the assurance I had been given about them meeting the later flight.

"Well now," came the sleepy drawl of the night clerk, "ah don' know anything 'bout all that, 'cept our driver's off duty since 'bout 'leb'n peeyem."

Fortunately, cab drivers know when the late flights arrive, so we found one to take us to the motel. As I walked up to the registration desk, I was greeted by the guy whom I had spoken to on the phone.

"Well now," he said, scratching his head, "y'all hung up s' fast that ah never did get t' tell yuh that all owah rooms are occupied."

"No, you don't understand," I replied. "We have a reservation for a suite, which I reconfirmed earlier this evening."

"Well now, all ah kin tell yuh is that all owah suites are taken," said the clerk. "Ah know that f' sure, 'cause ah checked in th' family that got th' last one."

"Could I speak to the motel manager?" I asked, biting my lip to keep control.

"Well now, he's at home, sleepin' rat about now ah'd guess," he answered.

"Well now," I said, biting even harder, "could you give me his phone number?"

"Cain't do that. He'd kill me f' sure."

"Then can I use your phone to make a local call," I said, to which he nodded just in time for me to avoid needing stitches on my lip.

"We have to call your brother-in-law," I said to Missy. She dialed their number, apologized for the call at what was now some time after one in the morning, and explained what happened.

"He'll call the manager at home. All we can do is wait," she said.

So we sat in the lobby and waited. A few minutes later, the phone at the reception desk rang and I watched as the clerk answered. He turned his back to us, cupping the receiver as he spoke in hushed but obviously nervous tones. He then left the desk and went to the elevator.

About fifteen minutes later, before the clerk had come back, a man entered the lobby from outside, rushing up to where we were sitting.

"You the folks ah'm supposed t' take t' the other motel?"

"Excuse me," I said. "I don't understand."

"Well, the motel manager jes' woke me up and tol' me t' get over here t' take some people to the other Holiday Inn 'cross town."

Before I could say another word, the elevator door opened and through the lobby marched the desk clerk, with suitcases in both hands, followed by what looked like a couple with four kids, all in their bathrobes, carrying smaller pieces of luggage, dolls, and, yes, a teddy bear.

"Harry," said the desk clerk handing the suitcases to the van driver and indicating the family behind him with a jerk of his head, "these here are th' ones yore drivin'."

"Wait a minute," I exclaimed, "you're not going to —"

"Ah'm doin' jes' what the boss tol' me," he said, picking

188

up our luggage. "Y' all kin follow me up and the maid'll be here in a few minutes t' clean up the suite."

As glad as we were to have the room, we felt really rotten about the people who were evicted. We kept telling ourselves it wasn't our fault. But we didn't sleep a wink.

Later that morning, the motel manager called to apologize, telling us he had no idea how the mix-up happened, promising to make it up to us, and inviting us to have breakfast on the house in their coffee shop. We hadn't eaten dinner the night before, so we were hungry and we took him up on this offer. As we sat in our booth waiting for our order, we felt that despite all the mishaps of the trip thus far, at least we were here together and no one except Missy's sister and her husband would be any the wiser.

Then I happened to glance outside toward the motel entrance. I blinked a few times as my eyes widened and my mouth fell open in absolute astonishment at what I was seeing.

"Oh my God, I don't believe it!" I blurted out as Missy looked over at me, alarmed that maybe I was ill.

"What?" she exclaimed. "What's the matter?"

"What the hell are they doing?" I almost shouted, pointing to the window behind her.

There, under the motel marquee, stood the manager proudly looking at the sign that a workman had just finished putting up in foot-high, bright red capital letters.

THE HOLIDAY INN WELCOMES ALLEN AND MISSY ROSENSHINE FROM BBDO

People who witnessed it probably wondered why someone would come running out of the motel, pointing at the marquee and yelling, *"Take it down!"*

And I'm sure the perplexed motel manager couldn't quite figure out the expression on my face when he asked, "Don't you want a picture of you and the missus in front of the sign?"

A Night at the Opera

After Bruce Crawford turned BBDO over to me as his successor and went on to run the Metropolitan Opera, he would occasionally invite Missy and me to join him and his wife, Chris, in his general manager's box. During the intermissions, we would go to Bruce's office for a glass of wine. It was an exceptional way to spend a night at the opera, but never more special than his invitation to join them on the evening of Luciano Pavarotti's fiftieth birthday, which Bruce had planned to commemorate with a midnight supper after Pavarotti's performance in *Tosca*.

Bruce's success in the worlds of both advertising and opera reflected his particular ability to run a business whose most critical employees were creative talents. On the one hand, Bruce has little patience for the patent nonsense regularly spouted by the self-important blowhards who pervade both the advertising and cultural scenes. At the same time, he has tremendous respect for the instincts, ingenuity, and inspiration of the many creative people on whom successful advertising as well as great opera depend. His understanding, tolerance, and management of their egos, their insecurities, and their inevitable moments of depression earned their trust. His recognition and celebration of their artistic brilliance brought him their devotion. The event he planned for Pavarotti was just such an example of Bruce's management style.

When the curtain fell on the final act of *Tosca,* and after Pavarotti had taken his curtain calls before a wildly applauding audience, Bruce escorted us backstage, which itself was an amazing experience. The singers had barely left the stage and the audience was still filing out of the opera house, but behind the curtain there was a beehive of activity. Stagehands had already begun to take down the massive and complex structures that decorate a Met production and had started putting up the sets for the next night's performance. It looked as though they were replacing one edifice with another of a totally different design, but constructing it on the same foundation. We knew that the part of the stage visible from the audience represented only a small fraction of the actual backstage area, but we had no idea of the tremendous size and scope of that operation. Hydraulic elevators and forklifts alternately removed and brought out huge pieces of scenery as scores of carpenters and other workmen first disassembled, and then began putting together, an entire opera's stage design and backdrops. It was a spectacularly coordinated, or more appropriately, choreographed performance in its own right. Missy and I watched like an enraptured audience for quite a while, until Bruce had to almost tear us away to go to his party for Pavarotti.

Many of the Met's foremost personalities had already gathered when we took our places at the dinner table. The only person missing was Pavarotti himself. For a while, we sipped our drinks and chatted, awaiting the honoree. No one seemed particularly concerned that he had not arrived, no doubt knowing that he did not live by the clock. And indeed, our patience was rewarded when he finally entered the room to a boisterous and exuberant welcome.

I was startled, however, to see that he was still in the full costume and make-up he wore in the last scene of *Tosca.* He strode into the room just as he had moved across the stage an hour before. His gestures and mannerisms were still the movements of the character he had depicted that evening. And he remained in that role for the rest of the night. The guest of honor at Bruce's gathering to mark the great tenor's birthday was far more Puccini's Mario Cavaradossi than Luciano Pavarotti.

And it struck me that this was a perfect example of how actors, who gain their fame and fortune by becoming people other than themselves, must often confuse their sense of who they are with the roles they play, to a point where they can even feel more confident and comfortable being someone other than themselves. I suppose it's a form of schizophrenia that is practically essential to giving a great theatrical performance. (And when you see and hear many actors actually being themselves, their alter egos are a blessing.)

Of course, for an opera singer, the voice supersedes the acting, which in earlier generations at the Met resulted in magnificent tenors like Jan Peerce and Richard Tucker striking the static poses of statues, only occasionally making a clumsy gesture or moving woodenly a few steps here or there as they sang their roles. But in more recent times, singers like Pavarotti and Placido Domingo added the full energy, emotion, and dynamic of dedicated acting to bring the fullness of their characters to life, essentially becoming actors as well as singers.

So it struck me that for this world-famous tenor, and a star even without the traditional physical attractiveness of a Hollywood leading man, it was far easier to appear at his party as Mario Cavaradossi than as Luciano Pavarotti. It would have been funny had it been a costume party, and perhaps for him, that's what it really was. But I felt a sad undertone to it.

And I'd guess it becomes even sadder as the limelight fades for someone whose life is defined by playing fictional characters, finally left to confront the stranger in the mirror.

Tagged Out

For years, Delta Air Lines was one of BBDO's biggest accounts. It was managed by our agency in Atlanta, and since I worked in New York, I didn't have too much contact with the client. But when I had reached an altitude high enough in the agency hierarchy for them to spot me, it came time for me to meet Delta's chief executive, Ron Allen.

In those years, Delta was enjoying great success as the airline overwhelmingly preferred by business travelers, the most frequent and profitable type of customer for any national carrier. Delta led the field with its reputation for better personal service, provided by what every survey showed were the most attentive and friendly ticket agents, flight attendants, and baggage handlers.

Ron had come up through the Delta ranks as an expert in employee relations. He played a significant part in building Delta's customer service strength and its resulting business growth, a career path that had led him to the top of the company. Their advertising had for years dramatized these competitive benefits and now Ron took a personal interest in how our ads and commercials depicted the role of Delta people in the airline's performance.

So off I went, attaché case in hand, to Delta headquarters

at Atlanta's Hartsfield Airport. My mission was simple — to show the Delta chief executive that our dedication and loyalty to his company was not just the concern of our Atlanta operation, but was shared by the headquarters management in New York, evidenced now by my personal interest and commitment. Ron should feel that his counterpart in his advertising agency had Delta red, white, and blue running through his veins.

While I had certainly learned something about showing the agency's fidelity and devotion to the top management of our clients, Delta presented a particular challenge to me personally. The company very much reflected the traditions of the South. Most of the management, including Ron, came from southern families and upbringing. The closest I came to that scene was an uncle who left the Bronx during the Depression and wound up running a grocery store in Chattanooga. Nevertheless, I was determined to be as courteous, as soft spoken, and as laid back as the prototypical "good ol' boy" — in other words, as little of a New Yorker as possible. But I wasn't going to attempt even one syllable of "down-home" syntax or pronunciation as some people do to avoid seeming effete to the ears of Southerners. (In the army, by some mystical form of linguistic osmosis, every kid from Brooklyn winds up calling cadence as though born and bred in Biloxi — *hut two three fo', yo' lef', yo' lef', yo' lef' rat lef' rat lef'.)*

The introduction was made by one of the Delta executives with whom we worked on a day-to-day basis. "Well now, we sho' are mighty happy t' have th' folks from BBDO heah t' talk 'bout owah bidness, Mistuh Chairmun," he drawled as we were ushered into Ron's office. "This heah's Allen Rosenshine, the heyad of BBDO fum New Yoke."

"Well, it's a pleasure to meet yuh, Allen," said Ron, who thankfully seemed to hail from somewhere closer to the Mason-Dixon Line than his manager.

"Thank you, Ron," I replied. "I appreciate you taking the time to meet with us. Delta and BBDO have a long and pro-

194

ductive history, and I want you to know that I will do everything I can to see it outlast us both. I wanted to hear firsthand what you think about the advertising we're running and what our priorities should be in our future work," I concluded. I then made a point of opening my attaché case, bringing out a pad, and putting pen in hand, poised to take notes.

"Well, it's good that yuh're here, Allen," he said, " 'cause there surely are a few things we need t' get done, so we've gotta have you an' your folks marchin' with us right up there behind the Delta flag."

Ron then proceeded to speak about the state of the business; how he thought Delta was performing versus American Airlines, their primary competitor; what we should be emphasizing in the advertising in the year ahead; their problems and opportunities in the near and long term; what he saw as the trends in the industry; and so on. It was an organized and comprehensive overview. And throughout it all, I took copious notes, writing as fast as I could and nodding my awareness of the issues as he worked his way through them.

"I'm glad to see yuh takin' all those notes, Allen," said Ron when he had finished. "It's not ever'body 'round here who listens 'fore they start runnin' off doin' their own thing."

"Well, thank you, Ron," I replied. "I'm not sure where the quote comes from, but I believe whoever said, 'You can't learn anything while you're talking,' had it right."

"Hey, ah like that one," he said. "Next guy comes in here yappin' just to hear himself talk, ah'm gonna lay that on 'im. So what d'yuh think about what I'm sayin'?" asked Ron.

"The truth is, Ron, I honestly don't know yet what I think," I answered. "I'd like to take some time with these notes I made and get back to you."

"Well, ah'll be," said Ron. "Been a long time since anyone looked me in the eye an' admitted they did'n' know somethin' an' wanted to go off an' think about it. You do that an' get back t' me."

"I sure will, Ron," I said, really feeling on a roll and very satisfied that I had accomplished my primary goal of saluting that Delta flag Ron had so picturesquely described. Having no more humble submissiveness left in me, I figured I couldn't do much more to impress Ron, so I thanked him again for his attention, closed my attaché case, and stood up to leave.

Ron came around from behind his desk and put a hand on my shoulder as we walked toward the door.

"Say, Allen, there is one thing you can do for me right now, 'fore yuh go," he said.

"Sure, Ron," I replied, "name it."

"Well, Allen," he said reaching into his pocket and taking out a luggage ID tag, "ah'd sure appreciate it if yuh'd take that *American* frequent flyer tag off your briefcase an' put this Delta tag on instead. Could yuh do that for me?"

It was a tribute to Ron's appreciation of our work that we kept the Delta account for many more years in spite our first encounter. And I was grateful that whenever he talked about that meeting, he always described it as the one where the head of his advertising agency sat in his office, taking notes. He never once reminded me of that tag on my attaché case.

Believe me, he didn't have to.

The Playboy

When John Sculley was my client running the Pepsi-Cola business, he invited me to accompany him to an event at Mount Vernon, the home of George Washington. It was scheduled on or about the due date for the birth of my first daughter. When I told John why I probably couldn't go, he of course understood but he urged me to come with him if it appeared that the delivery would be late.

It was to be a black-tie affair, well attended by businesspeople and politicians who I realized would be good for me to meet. And as John explained, he would be flying to Washington late that afternoon on a PepsiCo plane, so my joining him at the last minute would not be a problem for either of us.

At around noon on that day, my wife saw her obstetrician, who concluded that she would not give birth for a few days. So we decided that I should go since John planned to return very early the next morning. All told, I'd be away for about eighteen hours.

The event was every bit as upscale and chic as John had promised. Champagne was served at sunset on a rolling lawn overlooking the Potomac River. I met and mingled with CEOs, ambassadors, a cabinet member or two, senators and representatives, all of whom were, if not new business opportunities for

197

my agency, at least names worth dropping in conversation with clients and prospects.

At the announcement of dinner, I excused myself to call home, which I had promised to do every few hours. There was no answer but I saw no reason for concern, assuming that my wife had perhaps gone for a short walk as she often did, or might be visiting a neighbor. After the first course, I called again. And again, no answer. Because it was less than a half hour since the first call, I decided to wait another half hour before checking again. When my third call went unanswered, I started phoning around.

I called our doctor. Naturally, I got his answering service informing me that if this was an emergency, they would have him call me back. Those were not the days of cell phones and I had no idea what number to leave. I called the hospital and was informed that they had no record of my wife checking in. I called home again. No answer. Thinking our phone might be out of order, I called our next door neighbors, who said they hadn't seen her that evening. They rang our bell while I waited, but as with the phone, no answer. Now in full panic mode, I started calling our friends and anyone I could think of who might know where she was. After a few unproductive attempts, I finally learned that she had been taken to the hospital by a friend about two hours before, but his wife had not heard from him yet.

I called the hospital again and was told that no one by her name had checked in that evening. I explained that my wife had been brought in a couple of hours ago, but I had long ago learned the total futility of arguing with institutional incompetence. I knew I was wasting my breath. It was now about nine o'clock and I was in Washington socializing while my wife was giving birth to our first child. I found John's table and told him what was going on.

"Oh my God, I feel terrible that I brought you here," he anxiously responded. "Let me see if I can contact our pilots and we'll fly you back tonight. If not, we'll drive back. One way or the other," he concluded, "you'll be back in a few hours."

He quickly reached the PepsiCo pilots and we were soon on our way to Washington's National Airport. I had tried to convince John that none of this was his fault and that he should remain at the dinner. He was determined, however, to personally supervise my return to New York.

As we flew back, John again apologized, but despite my reminding him that our doctor had assured us my wife would not go into labor that night, he obviously felt guilty. Before we landed, he got up and spoke quietly to the flight attendant, who soon brought him two bottles of champagne.

"Here, at least take these to celebrate with when the baby is born," he said.

After being whisked from the airport by a waiting limo, I arrived at the hospital shortly after midnight. I ran past the chauffer into the lobby and rushed up to the receptionist.

"My wife was admitted earlier this evening," I exclaimed. "She's a maternity patient and might be delivering right now." I could not understand the look of total contempt she gave me as she looked me up and down, head to toe and back again.

"What's the name, playboy?" she sneered.

Playboy? I thought. And then I realized what she was looking at — a guy in a tuxedo, hopping out of his limousine, brandishing a bottle of champagne in each hand, deigning to interrupt his partying to show up in the middle of the night while his wife was giving birth. It was a good thing she didn't know that I had just flown in from Washington on a private jet or she might have really thought I was a total shit.

Much to John's and my relief, not to mention my wife's, the playboy's daughter was born later that morning. The doctor got none of the champagne.

The Marriage of Figenbaum

I grew up with Marty Figenbaum (not his real name for reasons that will become apparent). We went to school together, played ball together, hung out together, and through the years, had dinner together fairly regularly with our wives.

My father died when I was eleven years old, having lost a long battle with leukemia. My mother had a little money from the sale of his share of the small pharmacy he owned and ran with a partner. But she had to go back to work to maintain the reasonably comfortable middle-class lifestyle my father had been able to provide. As a result, when we weren't at school or on the ball field, I often spent time in Marty's house when I might otherwise have been home alone, my brother having finished college and taken a job out of town.

After college, Marty went to work in market research, eventually starting a company of his own. Since his was a field related to advertising, and in fact, we sometimes worked for the same clients, our friendship also often included talking about business in addition to sports, politics, and family, most of which had us laughing for one reason or another. In each other's company, we never took life too seriously.

You wouldn't have known it from his pleasant nature and usually jovial demeanor, but Marty's father was involved with illegal gambling. I once asked Marty what his father did for a living.

"He's a bookie," Marty answered, as though it was a perfectly natural thing. And we never discussed it further.

Perhaps from his interest in research, or influenced by his father's predilection for gambling, Marty liked to play the stock market. He was a day trader long before the Internet made it possible for anyone in America to get hooked on the Wall Street version of betting. His father always laughed about Marty's preoccupation with the stock listings in the newspapers.

"Gimme me the money and I'll put it on a game when I know how it's gonna turn out," his father would say. "The odds are a helluva lot better than playing the market."

But it wasn't that easy, even when the supposed fix was in. I remember watching a football game in which one of the teams was favored to win by more than twenty points. In the gambling world, a high point spread like that is a rigged game waiting to happen. Since it's far easier in any sport to let the other team score than it is to score yourself, it was common knowledge that a heavily favored, and therefore far better team, might control a game by allowing their opponents to get close but not win. This was done by bribing a star player or two on the favored team to play below their ability — not too obviously but just enough to allow the other team an occasional opportunity to score. Thus, the better team could still come out ahead, and the big-time gamblers who had paid off the stars would have bet heavily on the underdog and won as well.

However, in this particular football game, it seemed that no matter what the quarterback did to help the other team, they were so inept, they couldn't take advantage. He fumbled right at their feet but they couldn't recover the ball. He threw passes to the defenders instead of his own receivers but they just bounced off their hands. And when they finally got possession of the ball, their offense was so hopeless, the quarterback's defensive team, unaware of their leader's agenda, would re-cover fumbles and intercept passes, scoring again and again. At the end of the first half, the favorites, despite their quarter-back's increasingly blatant efforts to keep the score close, led by more than thirty points, well over the twenty they were not supposed to exceed.

I called Marty. "Ask your father what's going on," I said. "This one looks too obvious to be true."

"He's not happy," Marty replied. "He says there's a ton of money on the game but they can't just keep handing it to those clowns. Anyone can see what's goin' on. They're gonna have to play it straight in the second half."

So they won by even more than thirty points, proving that even a sure thing isn't always a sure thing and sometimes the wise guys have a bad day at the office.

But when Marty got around to getting married, his father was determined that his wedding reception was going to be a great day. The actual ceremony took place in another city where his wife's family lived, but his father had planned a gala event for the newlyweds in New York as soon as they returned from their honeymoon. There was only one small problem — after the relatives, the people on the invitation list were a *Who's Who* of the local gambling scene, likely to attract law enforce-ment observers and photographers. This would draw unwanted attention to Marty's father's undeclared, and therefore untaxed, net worth reflected by the opulent celebration he had in mind.

Thus, the friends and relatives of Marty and the new Mrs. Figenbaum would be received in the basement of a synagogue, in a remote and run-down area of the Bronx.

It was a scene even Hollywood would have trouble stag-ing. We entered the building from a dark and dingy street, walking through a dilapidated hallway, then down a dimly lit, narrow stairwell, the exit door opening into a huge room that, compared to its surroundings, was like entering a ballroom in Versailles. The tables were adorned with huge bouquets and

202

candelabra, surrounded by upholstered chairs. The linens, dishes, silverware, and glasses were worthy of royalty. The music came not from the typical trio of saxophone, guitar, and an electronic keyboard backed by synthetic drumbeats, but from an eight-piece band of tuxedo-clad musicians who actually sounded like they played for a living. (Yes, instead of foie gras, there was chopped chicken liver in the shape of a duck, lest anyone forget the heritage of the occasion. But the entrée of entrecôte bore no resemblance to brisket.)

It was totally surreal.

Excepting the venue, the evening must have cost a small fortune. But Marty's father would have no fear of anyone outside that room having the slightest idea of the affair's well-disguised opulence. After the last envelope had been modestly tucked into Marty's jacket pocket and the guests were ready to make their way up from the basement, out of the Bronx, and back to the world in which they actually lived, I stopped to thank his father for the party.

"I really wanted to throw it at the Waldorf," he said wistfully as we shook hands, "but in my business, that wouldn'a been too smart. How's *your* business?" he asked as an afterthought.

"Crazy," I answered. "But not as crazy as yours."

The Philadelphia Ad Club

After I became creative director of BBDO New York, I would occasionally get invitations to speak at various marketing and advertising events, which I almost always accepted since they generally provided opportunities to help build our business. The audiences usually included some combination of potential clients, people we might want to hire, and trade press reporters whose stories could provide positive publicity for our agency. So my objective was to develop a talk that would enable me to show off BBDO's best advertising, present our most successful case histories, and offer a vision of the business that would make our agency competitively attractive.

But to avoid being totally self-serving, I would try to tailor my presentation as much as possible to whatever theme the event was centered around and the context of the agenda. This necessitated some basic knowledge about the organization sponsoring the meeting, the other speakers and their topics, and so on.

Some speaking requests came from the major industry associations with which we were quite familiar and were always good venues for our agency, and therefore did not take much thought about whether or not to accept their invitations.

Others, such as a call I got from the Philadelphia Ad Club, required a little investigating.

"Well, as you know, Mr. Rosenshine," said the very pleasant woman who identified herself as the secretary of the club, "Philadelphia is the headquarters of many important companies and many advertising agencies, and our group holds luncheons with guest speakers to keep us up to date on what is going on in the business. It would be wonderful for us to have the creative director of a great agency like BBDO come and talk with us." Then she added a few more comments in praise of our work, assuring me that their membership would come out in force to hear me and suggesting a few alternate dates for my appearance.

Somehow, I just didn't feel right about offering the standard delaying response of "Let me think about it, and get back to you," which was almost always preparatory to then turning down the request for some trumped-up but plausible reason. The woman was so enthusiastic, so accommodating, so complimentary, so nice, that I found myself agreeing to a date. And after all, I thought, in spite of jokes like "First prize is a week in Philadelphia, second prize is two weeks," it is nonetheless a major city with good business to be done there. I knew from appearing at other ad clubs in cities such as Detroit, where virtually all the American automotive business resides, or San Francisco, home of many major corporations, that this could be beneficial to BBDO. I also remembered the Denver Ad Club, where I had spoken very reluctantly because the city doesn't immediately leap to mind as pregnant with business possibilities. But I had been happily surprised by a large, welcoming, and highly appreciative audience that generated good press coverage. I figured Philadelphia might equally be worth my while.

So I committed to appear at a luncheon of the Philadelphia Ad Club to be held in one of the larger downtown hotels. I prepared accordingly, carefully selecting the advertising that would most appeal to a typical ad club audience of advertising and media people, featuring our most prominent and impressive clients, and building a talk around the importance of creating advertising that would promote a company's brands through establishing a strong appeal to the consumer's mind, heart, and way of life. I worked and reworked my speech, trimming it down to a reasonable after-lunch length, strategically interspersing our most emotional, humorous, and entertaining commercials to keep the audience alert and attentive to my message. And I found a few ways to inject some ingratiating comments about the similarity of our communications mission despite the differences in the size of our respective agencies in the New York and Philadelphia markets.

As I boarded the train on the morning of my appearance, I felt quite good about the show I had prepared. I arrived at the hotel shortly before noon to set up the audio-visual equipment, check out the podium lighting, microphone and sound system, and familiarize myself with the room in general. The event was posted on the hotel directory and I went directly to the listed meeting room.

When I opened the door, I was greeted by a jaw-dropping surprise.

The room was half the size of my office, with *one* table of ten set for lunch, a somewhat flimsy pull-up screen on a tripod (these were still the days before videotape), and an elderly, elegantly dressed lady turning the power switch of the film projector on and off to no apparent avail.

"Hello, I'm Doris Blake, secretary of the club and you must be Mr. Rosenshine," she said in her now familiar sweet voice, as she flicked the projector switch again. "Oh dear," she sighed, "it doesn't seem to be working. I hope that won't be too big a problem."

"Well, it's, uh, hardly ideal," I managed to stammer, as the shock of the overall scene began to set in. "I had hoped to show some of our work to your, um, ah, membership," I said, looking balefully at the lone table.

"Well, it's Mrs. Whitmore's projector, so maybe she'll be able to get it to work when she arrives with the other ladies," she said.

"The, uh, other *ladies*?" I said, now just beginning to realize the extent of the debacle.

"Yes, I think I hear them coming down the hall right now," said Mrs. Blake with a broad smile. "You should be very proud to know that our entire membership will be here for your speech, including Mrs. Wilburton, who is still on crutches from her broken hip."

"All nine of you?" I said, with another quick glance at the place settings.

"Yes indeed," beamed Mrs. Blake. "We love to watch advertising on the TV and to have someone so important from such a big agency come to speak to us. And I can tell you," she said, drawing a deep breath and looking at me triumphantly, "that doesn't happen every day."

"I'm sure not," I replied, now hopelessly resigned to a lunch that at least would be one to remember.

The next day, when our president asked me how things had gone at my Philadelphia Ad Club presentation, I answered as a good ad man should.

"Standing room only," I replied.

Minimum Wages

Many observers of marketing and advertising, and in fact, many practitioners in client and agency companies alike, concede that it is usually difficult, if not impossible, to determine the return on investments made to promote brands via traditional commercials and ads in mass media. Since time and a variety of other stimuli ordinarily intervene between a consumer's exposure to an advertising message and the actual purchase of the brand advertised, it becomes problematic to effectively measure any causality between the events. Some forms of marketing communications such as direct response, in which consumers react directly to specific approaches, or more recently, the Internet, which allows new methods of interactivity between sellers and buyers, make it possible to reasonably measure the economic benefits of the costs incurred. But the vast majority of global advertising expenditures still cannot be accurately or consistently related to any revenue or profit they might help generate.

So there is an understandably ongoing debate as to how much money to spend on advertising, and whether particular tactics in creating ads and commercials are worth what they cost. Intangibles such as the value of using famous actors, entertainers, or sports figures to either specifically endorse a brand or to appear as performers in advertising, are always a matter of continuous discussion, especially considering the very high premiums usually demanded by star talent. And it is generally only well after the contracts have been agreed, the advertising produced and run, and the big names supporting the big brands have met all their commitments that any intelligent assessment of the deal is possible.

For a company unaccustomed to spending heavily on the production of advertising, in addition to the media costs in delivering their messages to potential customers, the idea of writing checks in the millions of dollars to Hollywood personalities, singers, athletes, and assorted other subjects of popular adoration, who will neither produce nor deliver any product to market, is a very difficult proposition.

This was the case with one of BBDO's largest and longest-standing clients when we proposed using a star of considerable magnitude to shine his light on their brand.

As if the problem of convincing a reticent client to invest substantially for indefinable results is not enough, there are issues posed by the personality that must also be addressed. Their egos are measured by how much they are paid to perform in a film, in a show, on an album, on the ball field, or wherever. Leaving aside the private planes to jet them to a filming, the limousines in which they must travel, the luxury trailers that serve as their dressing rooms on location, the hotel suites that house them overnight, and the added cost of the entourage that invariably accompanies them, the basic question is always how much should they be paid to do the advertising.

Imagine a business negotiation in which the buyer has no idea of how much the purchase is realistically worth, while the seller's objective is to be paid as much or more than anyone else has earned in any similar deal. There is no logical starting point for the bargaining. Reason rarely prevails.

Having written a campaign to suit a particular personality, we were on the hook to deliver him — unfortunately to a client who usually paid performers in their commercials at basic union rates, a very small fraction of the fee we had fore-warned them would be the minimum we'd have to pay. The talent agent informed us that his star expected three million dollars, and that for only one year. Further discussion bogged down at two million, which they insisted could not be a penny less, and our client simply refused to consider. Realizing that two million was a number they demanded for ego and public relations purposes, we convinced our client to offer it, but for two years instead of one, with the second year and the second million dollars cancelable by either party. If the campaign was working, it would be worth it. And the talent would get it without having to do anything more than agree to let the commercials run. In any event, a second year's commitment from both sides could still be renegotiated.

But that's when the ego and numbers game had only just gotten started. Because that's when our client informed us that they couldn't agree to the contract without first shooting and testing the commercials with consumers to provide their board of directors with some justification for the expense.

"In other words," said the talent agent, "you expect my guy, a bona fide star in Hollywood and Las Vegas, to *audition* to do your commercials? Lemme tell you something, Allen," he went on in a tone that left little doubt where he stood, "I wouldn't insult him with that even if I thought he wouldn't fire me on the spot for bringing it to him. Tell your client to fuck off. We've got nothing further to talk about."

Besides not telling the client any such thing, I hated the thought of losing this campaign. Our people had written it just for this guy and I believed it would be a big sales success for the brand. And we had come so close to a deal that would have made it happen. So I stalled the client, reporting for the next few days that we were still working to get an agreement that in-cluded testing, which was at least half true, since I was indeed trying even if our star's agent was not.

And then it struck me.

"How much does he get when he shoots a movie, appears on TV, or does a live show?" I called and asked the agent. "In other words, how much does he make when he's actually working?"

"I'd say he averages about two hundred fifty grand a week," he answered.

"Okay, here's a deal I think you can take to him," I said. "We'll pay him that for *two days*."

"How do you figure that?" said the agent, somewhat incredulously.

"We'll pay him that much to shoot the campaign, which will take two days," I explained, "and then we'll test it off the air. We do it with private showings to specially selected audiences. Nobody sees it on TV. If it doesn't work, it never runs and he keeps the two fifty. If it works, we've already agreed on the deal to run it. So you're already getting him more than he usually makes," I concluded excitedly, "and for two days' work, he could wind up making two million bucks."

The next day, we convinced the client that the financial risk was worth the potential reward. And our star was convinced that he was worth a million dollars a day.

Perfectly logical, no?

Commuting First Class

Not long after I joined BBDO, I moved to Mamaroneck, a suburban community about twenty-five miles north of New York City. My first wife had recently given birth to our son and we were looking for a more hospitable way of life than the city offered back then. Since my wife had stopped working and my salary was still fairly modest, we were also interested in making our housing dollar go further, so we bought a two-bedroom co-op and left our one-bedroom rental in Manhattan.

Another financial consideration was the proximity of our new apartment to the commuter railroad station. It had to be walking distance because we did not want to spend money on a second car for me to drive to and from the station.

We had investigated the demographics of the area to insure that we would be among people our age with young kids and that the town offered a public school system that could provide a decent education in a safe environment. Mamaroneck seemed to meet all our requirements and became the first place either of us had lived outside the boroughs of the Big Apple.

On the first Monday morning of our lives in Mamaroneck, I left for work, making the fifteen-minute walk from our apartment to the train station. It was a pleasant day in the early fall as the leaves were just starting to turn the colors of the season. The air, the streets, and the entire ambiance all seemed to validate our move from the city.

I got to the station about ten minutes before the train was due, in spite of the many stories I had already heard about the perennially late trains, which along with generally terrible service, seemed to be hallmarks of the commuter line. It had been the one subject of concern I had about the move. I didn't want to spend more than a half hour each way on the train, which was the railroad's scheduled time for the trip. But I figured nothing was perfect, and more and more people were moving from the city to the suburbs even if the commuter service was a problem. They seemed quite willing to put up with it.

I bought my first monthly round-trip ticket between Mamaroneck and Grand Central Station, and went out to the southbound track to await the first commuter ride of my new life in suburbia. I thought when the train arrived in the city, the first car would be closest to the exit, so I headed for the front end of the platform.

There I found my second reason to worry.

With all the research I had done on the population of the town, it struck me as odd that almost all the men waiting for the train were older than me — in fact, much older, and far better and more expensively dressed. Even then, I didn't have much hair but what little I had was not gray like the hair on practically all the heads I could see not covered by fancy fedoras. Double-breasted suits in dark pinstripes, white shirts, and solid or striped silk ties seemed very much the uniform of the men of Mamaroneck. I stood out in a still summery, blue-and-white-striped seersucker suit with its characteristically rumpled look.

Uh oh, I thought, *where are all the guys who have little kids and are still looking up the corporate ladders? If anyone in this crowd has preschoolers at home, it must be a visit from their grandchildren.*

213

My ominous reverie was interrupted by the arrival of the train, the first car coming to a stop where the country club crowd and I had gathered. My next surprise came from the doorway of the first car where a porter, clad in a white waiter's jacket stepped out and stood aside, greeting each of us as we boarded.

"Good morning, sir, and welcome aboard," he repeated.

Well, I don't know what all the bitching is about, I said to myself. *This seems like pretty good service to me.*

It only got better once inside the car. Instead of the typical rows of three-seaters one would expect, half the comfortably air-conditioned car had linen-covered tables, each with four chairs around them, with the remainder of the car having upholstered armchairs lined up with their backs to the windows, facing the center of the car. At some of the tables, people were playing bridge. Then, as the train pulled out of the station, the porter, whom I now realized was actually a steward, came by offering each of us a glass of orange juice.

It occurred to me that I might either be dreaming or more likely on the wrong train. I felt this couldn't be a commuter train renowned for terrible service, and I certainly couldn't see any up-and-coming young executives with their attaché cases open, priming themselves for their first meeting of the morning. On the contrary, these men were all casually reading the *Wall Street Journal,* and from the bits of conversation I could overhear, complaining vociferously about Hubert Humphrey, who was then running a close race for president against their obvious favorite, Richard Nixon.

Maybe, I thought, *these are a bunch of lawyers and bankers on their way to Washington.* As the steward passed by, I stopped him to ask, "Excuse me, but is this the 7:45 train to Grand Central?"

"Yes, sir," he replied, but before continuing on his way, he looked me over very carefully and then reached slowly into the pocket of his white jacket, withdrawing a small card and handing it to me. The embossed script has been emblazoned in my memory ever since.

You are seated in a private club car for members only. You may be more comfortable farther back in the train.

The suggestion on the card turned out only half right. I was indeed more at ease among more demographically and socially suitable traveling companions, but not at all more comfortable in standing-room-only cars where not having a seat was almost preferable to the hard-backed benches, and where you activated the air-conditioning by prying open, if you could, the usually jammed and always filthy windows.

To be fair, the commuter trains have since become far more modern and far less class conscious. But it occurred to me many years later, having risen in my company to a point of entitlement to a chauffer-driven car to bring me to and from the office, that I may have been to some extent subconsciously motivated by the desire to shove that card up some private car member's ass.

The Silence of the Legends

Shortly after becoming creative director of BBDO New York, I had the opportunity to meet and mingle with some of the legendary leaders of the advertising business. The occasion was a book party hosted by BBDO for one of our more prominent people, John Caples. He had written a book, *They Laughed When I Sat Down to Play,* a title taken from a direct response ad he had written, promoting the ease and speed with which people could learn to play the piano when nobody would have thought them capable of it. This type of advertising got its name from the ability of the consumer, by using a coupon or phone number, to respond directly to the advertiser to purchase the product or service being offered. Caples's theories about this kind of advertising were the basis for his book.

Perhaps the best known of the attendees was David Ogilvy, who had written one of the most famous books about advertising, *Confessions of an Advertising Man,* and had established a major agency bearing his name. Everyone in the business knew who he was. Clients, agencies, and the trade press alike regularly quoted from his book, most often alluding to his rules for successful advertising.

While I certainly had to admire his accomplishments, I was less impressed than others with some of his ideas, espe-

216

cially the notion that effective advertising had to follow Ogilvy's inexorable mandates. I don't much believe in "always" or "never" as a way of living, much less as a call to creativity in communications. But rules certainly make things easier in complex situations, which was obviously appealing to Ogilvy's disciples.

I recall an article I read by him when I first started out as a junior copywriter, in which he wrote about his personal approach to preparing an ad for a client. He emphasized the need to remain objective about one's own writing and to avoid being satisfied with early drafts. He made a big point that he would finish an ad and then not look at the copy he had written for a couple of weeks to see if he would still like it later as much as he did in his usual early burst of enthusiasm. I thought that made sense except for one small detail — if it was me taking two weeks to submit the copy for one of my assignments, I'd get fired. (I suppose you have more latitude when your name is on the agency's door.)

Anyway, there I stood in a roomful of advertising greatness, not wanting to miss the chance to be able to tell people that I had chatted with David Ogilvy. So, fortified by a first glass of wine and armed with a second, I demurely approached him.

"Excuse me, Mr. Oglivy," I began, "my name is Allen Rosenshine and I'm the new creative director at BBDO."

He slowly lowered his pipe from his mouth, looked me straight in the eye, squinting slightly and cocking his head to one side. I took all that as the mannerisms of his well-known British upbringing and felt I had his attention.

"I wanted to take this opportunity to introduce myself," I continued, intending some flattery, "since you are a leader of creativity in our business. Your career has certainly helped make the creative work our most important asset," I concluded, fully expecting a handshake and a few accompanying words of encouragement.

217

He glanced at my extended hand, otherwise ignoring it, pinched his eyes almost shut and furrowed his brow in an expression of unmistakable annoyance. (It occurred to me later that maybe he was just constipated.) He held the pose for what seemed an excruciatingly long time, at last taking a long, deep breath.

"Wot?" he finally exclaimed, before he turned and shuffled away.

I never had another chance to meet David Ogilvy. Then again, I never looked for one.

The Phosphate Syndrome

In marketing and advertising, a great deal of money is spent on research to learn what consumers think, how they act, and most important, what would motivate people not just to use a particular product, but to choose one specific brand over all the others. Advertising agencies and research companies follow a constant process of devising and utilizing interviewing methodologies designed to help understand what consumers want and how best to position a given brand as the competitively unique solution they will therefore repeatedly purchase.

It's instructive to note that the issue is a consumer "want" rather than a "need." This is not just splitting hairs over definitions. In fact, there is a huge and important difference. A former chief executive of BBDO, Tom Dillon, used to say, "The only things a consumer *needs* is about fifteen hundred calories a day and a warm place to sleep." Allowing for his obvious hyperbole, his point was that a "need" is a requirement, while a "want" is a wish but not a necessity. The business of building brands through marketing and advertising, he professed, is the business of understanding, catering to, and admittedly sometimes stimulating or even creating consumer "wants."

Many unsympathetic observers have turned this into the accusation that the objective of advertising is to convince people to buy all kinds of things they don't need. Ironically, Tom would surely have agreed. Nobody needs a deodorant, a computer, or an off-road vehicle. They are not life-supporting products that qualify as "needs." They are, however, examples of life-enhancing innovations that in one way or another distinguish the human condition. We are the one species capable of reaching beyond just the needs of Darwinian survival. Not even our closest relatives among the primates enjoy the art, literature, and music of their fellow apes. At the end of the evolutionary day, we are the ones defined by our "wants." It also takes advertising to inform us how best we can satisfy them.

Those who disparage the notion of "truth in advertising," should better understand that to distort what a product can or will do to satisfy consumers' physical or psychological "wants" would result in people buying it only once, which would certainly destroy any brand in short order. To paraphrase a warning from one of the true creative geniuses of advertising, Bill Bernbach, the worst thing advertising can do is overpromise. In other words, advertising that lies is ultimately advertising that fails.

The purpose of market research is to uncover what consumers want so that we can communicate how our clients' brands can best fulfill their wishes. As it turns out however, consumers are often less than truthful in their responses to our research. This is because people will usually protect their self-images rather than admit to behavior that might seem selfish or anti-social.

Major manufacturers in multibillion dollar product categories can thus be led astray. In laundry detergents, for example, they rushed to develop and advertise non-phosphate cleaning products in reaction to a spate of publicity that phosphates pollute our streams and rivers. But it wasn't just the words of the environmentalists that goaded them into action. More critically, when consumers were asked about their willingness to necessarily sacrifice some of the cleaning efficacy that phosphates provided in order to have a product that would produce less pollution, they responded overwhelmingly that they would happily use non-phosphate detergents.

Unfortunately, that's what they *said,* not what they *did.*

Because in fact, they were not ready to accept less than the whiter-than-white, brighter-than-bright clothes they had come to expect. In the research, they only said they would, because to have responded otherwise would have made them look thoughtless and unconcerned about the welfare of our waterways. In the privacy of their own shopping carts, they chose the brands that gave them what they really wanted — the cleanest possible clothes.

Whether you consider this behavior rational (acting according to what you actually want) or irrational (saying one thing but doing another), this "phosphate syndrome" exists just as much in life as in laundry. Most men will probably tell you that the way a woman *looks* is not as important as who she really *is*. Women, of course, know better, as the billions of dollars they spend every year on fashion and cosmetics certainly suggest. And how often do we hear women say it's not important how much money a man spends to show them they care, but rather how well men *understand* them? That would certainly come as news to Tiffany or De Beers. On a more lofty plane, most Americans would ardently agree that voting is the most important responsibility of a citizen in a democracy. But where are they on Election Day?

People most often say what they want others to hear, so the business of figuring out and satisfying their real desires can create some pretty confusing challenges in marketing and advertising. The reasons consumers subscribe to one brand or another are as complex as people themselves. The "phosphate syndrome" can, and often does, drive marketers to completely counterproductive conclusions, contributing to some monumental business disasters in major product categories.

Remember the Edsel — an ugly, snout-nosed, lump of a

car named after a member of the Ford family, whom no one had ever heard of? Or Billy Beer — a watery-tasting brew that America would ostensibly want to guzzle because it was made by a president's ne'er-do-well brother? Or New Coke — a radical change in the taste of one of the world's most popular drinks largely because Pepsi was thumbing its nose at Coke in its advertising?

In fact, the vast majority of new products brought to the showrooms and supermarkets of America actually fail, at least in part, because of consistently faulty research.

Isn't that crazy?

Staring Into Ol' Blue Eyes

I met Frank Sinatra twice, although it would be more accurate to say that I encountered him, since our meetings were mostly a matter of being in the same place at the same time. Both occasions were in their own ways very disconcerting, but for totally different reasons.

The first time took place in La Grenouille, one of New York's, and no doubt the world's, finest French restaurants. My wife, Missy, and I were having dinner with a client and his wife when I noticed at a table directly facing us, Sinatra among a small group of people. One of them, based on his size, demeanor, and lack of female accompaniment, appeared to be his bodyguard, made further apparent during our meal by my occasional glances toward their table, which confirmed that he was neither eating nor drinking. He just sat there, in no way participating in the animated conversation going on around him.

More than once, in fact quite often, I noticed that Sinatra would look over in our direction, or more specifically at Missy, whose beauty has turned many heads, even among men accustomed to the company of very attractive women. At first, I must admit I was actually flattered that he seemed taken by her looks. Then I began to think, *Maybe he figures I'd be no match for him in her eyes.*

It wouldn't have been the first time that other men had hit on her regardless of my presence. I remembered a client who had a reputation for showing more than professional interest in women from both his and our organizations. He came on to Missy at a resort where I gave a speech at a conference of the marketing and advertising directors of the various brands he supervised. He had cornered her at a cocktail reception, suggesting in no uncertain terms that she could do a lot better by spending the night with him instead of me. Fortunately, Missy didn't tell me about this until some years later when he was no longer a client. Had she told me at the time, I would have been caught between the "rock" of confronting him and making it untenable for BBDO to work on his account, and the "hard place" of pretending he hadn't made more than a passing pass at my wife.

But now it wasn't just some horny businessman, with his wife back in suburbia and his brain between his legs, apparently taking an interest in Missy. *Or maybe,* I thought, *I'm imagining things. Maybe I'm reading too much into Sinatra doing nothing more than looking at a beautiful woman. Maybe I should just relax and enjoy the food and wine at a great restaurant, and stop worrying whom those blue eyes were staring at.*

Which I had finally convinced myself to do, when Sinatra and his party, having finished their meal, stood up to leave. I looked at Sinatra. He looked at Missy. He came around his table and walked directly up to ours, standing right behind our guests, looking straight down at Missy. His bodyguard, right next to him, now appeared far bigger than when he sat at their table. I thought I ought to say something, but none of the choices that flashed through my mind seemed appropriate at that moment.

What are you looking at? That seemed a little aggressive

with a real-life Luca Brasi standing there. *Is there something I can do for you?* I could just imagine Sinatra's retort.

And throughout it all, Missy, the object and cause of this confrontation, chatted away with my client's wife, as though nothing was happening, which for her was exactly the case, since she is oblivious to the famous faces of the world. (If the president of the United States walked up to her and extended his hand, she would most likely say, "Hi, do I know you?") Finally, after some time between a few seconds and forever, she gave a cursory glance up at Sinatra and immediately turned back to her conversation.

That ended it. Sinatra abruptly walked away and left the restaurant. I wish I could say that I had backed him down, but it was clearly Missy's lack of recognition that in fact dismissed him.

It would be some years until the second time I was in the same room with Sinatra, this time at a private party in the penthouse of a Las Vegas hotel. It was a reception honoring the retirement of our client, Lee Iacocca. The main event had been a spectacular show in the field house of the UNLV basketball team, attended by thousands of Chrysler dealers, employees, and suppliers from all over the world. The highlight of the show was a surprise appearance by Sinatra, a personal friend of Lee's, singing a version of "My Way" rewritten to highlight the achievements in Lee's career. Because he had arrived at the last moment and didn't have time to rehearse, Sinatra seemed to have some trouble finding his position on the complicated multidirectional stage and reading the monitors that displayed the lyrics. But even with a false start and some fumbling, he delivered the tribute to tumultuous applause. After the show, a selected group of guests, including a few of us from BBDO, had been invited to the hotel for cocktails and dinner with Lee.

I didn't know who would be at the party but when I arrived, most of the guests, including numerous Hollywood personalities, had already assembled. I ordered a drink and munched on some hors d'oeuvres as I made my way toward the sound of a piano playing some familiar Sinatra standards. And there, sitting on the piano bench alongside the pianist, was Sinatra, his Jack Daniels in hand, singing along, but almost inaudibly. He didn't even seem to realize that, incredibly, *no one* was listening to him. He would sing a line or two and then appear to lose his concentration, coming back to the lyrics now and again in an obviously disjointed and unfocused rendition of his song. At first I thought he might be drunk. But then I realized he was *lost*. Sinatra had no idea where he was or why he was there.

At dinner, I was seated near him and he seemed no more aware of his surroundings than before. Finally, before the entrée was served, his companion took him gently by the arm and unobtrusively led him out of the room. Since they did not return, I assumed he had been taken home.

And I thought how ironic it was that in La Grenouille, because of Sinatra, I was unsettled, bemused, and at the mercy of a situation over which I had no control.

And years later, as I again looked on, so was Sinatra.

Buddy, Can You Spare a Hundred?

Sooner rather than later, New Yorkers are faced with someone asking for a handout. These panhandlers come in all shapes, sizes, and varieties — from filthy, smelly, unkempt bums accosting you for spare change, to people with their hard-luck stories hand lettered on makeshift signs, claiming everything from being homeless, to out of work, to whatever might move you to reach in your pocket.

No doubt some of these tales of woe are true and their victims deserving of help. But it's an equally sure thing that many of them are scams. Once, while riding the subway, I watched a man wearing sunglasses, with a white cane in one hand and a paper cup in the other, tapping his way through the car, his head slightly raised, turning back and forth as though listening intently in the classic manner of the blind.

"A little help?" he said, as he slightly jostled one passenger and extended his cup. "Anything ya can spare?" he asked another. "Can ya help a guy out?" he pleaded with someone as he approached where I was standing in front of the door leading to the next car. When he was just a few feet from me, I still hadn't moved out of his path, and with no one left between me and the door, he stopped tapping his cane, stuck his cup in his coat pocket, and turned his head directly toward me.

"Get the fuck outta my way!" he snarled under his breath, pushing past me and grabbing the door handle.

But this was nothing compared to the little swindle that one of our agency's account executives encountered one snowy morning while walking through Grand Central Station on his way to the office. He was stopped by a man neatly groomed, and dressed in a hat, scarf, topcoat, and galoshes, carrying an attaché case in one hand and a small suitcase in the other. The man had been looking around with an air of desperation as he approached.

"Excuse me, but could you help me for a minute?" he asked urgently but politely.

"Sure," our guy answered, assuming that the man needed directions. But instead of asking anything further, he put down his bag, reached into his attaché case, took out a business card, and handed it to my friend.

"Look, as you can see from my card, my name is Michael Wilson and I work for McCann-Erickson here in the city. I'm supposed to be in Boston on business at lunchtime but all the shuttle flights have been canceled because of the weather, so I'm trying to catch a train. But I was in such a rush, I ran out of my apartment without my wallet and I can't get to my office without missing the train. My money and credit cards are at home," he continued, now somewhat breathlessly, "but I need to buy a ticket and catch a cab to my meeting. I know it's a lot to ask but if you can lend me, say a hundred bucks, and give me your card, you'll have it back first thing tomorrow."

"Well, I guess so," said our account man, then adding as an afterthought as he looked at the card he'd been handed, "Say, it says you're an account executive. What kind of business is this McCann-Erickson in?"

"Insurance," came the instant reply.

"Wrong!" said our account man triumphantly. McCann is one of the biggest ad agencies in the world. But nice try, fella," he added with a laugh as he stepped past him to continue on his way.

When he got to his office, he called Wilson (whose real name is not important) at McCann and introduced himself.

"By any chance," he asked, "did you recently give money to some guy who told you he had forgotten his wallet and said he was running to catch a train?"

"Yeah, this morning in Grand Central. But how did . . . oh shit," he moaned as he suddenly understood. "He gave you *my* card."

"Yep. You may want to call the guy whose card you have and tell him not to hold his breath waiting for his money."

"Yeah, " said Wilson. "I can't believe I was so dumb."

"Hey, don't feel so bad," said our account executive. "Like they say in the mob, 'It wasn't personal. It was just business.' "

The One That Got Away

In 1986, when three major advertising agencies merged in what *Time* magazine headlined as "The Big Bang" in the industry, it was the first time *three* companies in our business (and maybe any business) had come together. Considering the potential clashes of ego, turf, titles, compensation, client conflicts, and general angst the traditional two-agency merger entailed, this was indeed big news. When most of the dust had settled (it's the nature of mergers that there will always be some of it lingering in the air long after the deal is done), two of the three agencies had been combined, and the third, BBDO, remained organizationally unchanged, except that it was now owned by, and reported to, a new holding company, Omnicom Group.

Beyond all the personal and business issues that the three managements faced during the negotiations, the most critical concern was the possible loss of clients due to competitive conflicts that would exist when the three agencies came under one corporate roof. In the advertising business, it would be highly unusual for one company to have competing companies as clients. This problem, for reasons none of us in the agencies can fathom, is not shared to nearly the same extent by lawyers, accountants, consultants, or other service professions that provide strategic counsel in even more sensitive areas of confidential information than marketing and advertising. In any event, when two agencies merge, there is an expected fallout of revenue from departing clients who would not tolerate a competitor being served by their agency.

The problem for Omnicom was considerably compounded by our deal involving not two but three client rosters. Our rationale for trying to convince concerned clients that their confidentialities would be protected was that we would keep the reorganized agencies totally separate, with completely different managements and staffs, each located in their own, unshared offices. They would operate completely independently from each other as subsidiaries of Omnicom. And we hoped that clients in question would also appreciate the quality of work they had been receiving to their satisfaction before the merger, and would therefore prefer to keep the same people and resources on their brands, rather than have to find a new agency.

The standard rule of thumb in analyzing the profit potential of an agency merger was to assume that approximately ten percent of the combined revenue would be lost from departing clients. Any more than that would usually jeopardize the financial viability of the newly formed enterprise. In the case of Omnicom, we were able to retain significantly more competing clients than we expected.

But in the automotive product category, we had no possibility of keeping all our businesses. Each of the three agencies had a major car account (Chrysler, Volkswagen, and Honda) and there would only be two agencies left to serve them after the merger. In addition, those being the years of intense competition between American and Japanese car companies that the imports were clearly winning, Chrysler, our BBDO client, would under no circumstances tolerate Honda as part of the mix. Lee Iacocca was, however, prepared to accept VW since he did not consider Germany as great a threat in the U.S. car market as Japan.

However, it wasn't to be quite that easy.

Chrysler insisted on rewriting our contract with them to include new and very specific protections against any possible breaches of confidentiality, which included, among many other stipulations, that because our sister agency would continue working for VW, no BBDO employee could move to them immediately after leaving our agency. We argued that this went well beyond any safeguard they could enjoy with any other agency since it would be quite impractical, if not impossible, to enforce between agencies that were not owned, as we were, by a single holding company. But when Lee was convinced of what he wanted, he was usually not disposed to debate.

The new contract became yet another windfall for our respective lawyers. As is always the case, almost every word, every phrase, every sentence, every punctuation mark, every "wherefore" and "whereas" between the party of the first part and all other parties of all other parts, was poured over as the billable hours accumulated. Eventually, we signed the revised deal so that no one from BBDO would be able to work at our sister agency, which would retain VW, for a stipulated period from the time they left us.

And then a funny thing happened.

Literally within the next week, John Damoose, the top marketing and advertising executive at Chrysler, and our most important day-to-day client, resigned his position and the following week joined another company in the same capacity. The company he now kept was — you guessed it — *Volkswagen*.

As you might have also guessed, I resisted the temptation to point out the irony to Mr. Iacocca.

The Birth of a Slogan

The slogan or theme line of an advertising campaign encapsulates the brand message in what should be a very short, memorable, and distinguishing phrase. After years of creating a variety of themes for Pepsi, each a restatement of the ongoing "Pepsi Generation" idea, linking the brand to the attitudes, trends, and issues of the times, we needed to incorporate a more competitive notion to further differentiate Pepsi from Coke. The new slogan was to be in keeping with a major change in the style of Pepsi advertising, moving it from songs and vignettes highlighting a youthful enthusiasm for life, to the more edgy world of teen music and entertainment, of which the Michael Jackson commercials were the first to run.

In addition, the new theme had to maintain the brand equity built by the previous two decades of advertising, while suggesting the taste superiority of Pepsi over Coke. This had been established by a highly successful promotion called "The Pepsi Challenge." Consumers tried both products without knowing which was which, with the majority repeatedly choosing Pepsi as tasting better. Communicating both notions was a lot to ask of one pithy and poignant phrase.

With no days remaining before our date at Pepsi to present our new ideas to their chief executive, Roger Enrico, we hadn't come up with a line that we liked. As Phil Dusenberry, our creative leader, and I drove to PepsiCo headquarters, we were desperately revisiting thoughts we had previously rejected, hoping to find one that we could make better. After a fruitless half hour, and with not much time left before we arrived, we were about to resign ourselves to telling Roger that we didn't have the answer. But assuming he liked the direction of the commercials we would present, we'd assure him we could solve the slogan in the time we still had before the finished work would be presented to their bottlers — the hundreds of companies that actually made and distributed Pepsi in their local markets across the country. Given the importance of the slogan in motivating not just consumers but also this vital network of local sales organizations that also funded the advertising, we knew not having it in hand would disappoint Roger and perhaps even unnerve him since he had already invested millions of dollars to bring Michael and Pepsi together for this new campaign. We could only hope he would have his usual faith in our ability to still get it right.

"You know, Phil," I said, checking my watch, "we're a little early and we can always say we got stuck in traffic, so why don't we cruise around and give it another shot. We've been hoping for that flash of brilliance to come up with the line but maybe if we went at it more analytically, we could think of something to at least show Roger we have a line that works."

"Okay, Allen, but what's 'analytically' supposed to mean?" said Phil, in his usual hurry to get to the point.

"Look, we've gotta recall the 'generation' theme," I began, "we've gotta remind people of the taste tests where they chose Pepsi over Coke, and we've gotta create some excitement around Michael and his music and the new approach we're taking."

"Yeah, so?" said Phil, now getting impatient.

"So let's try something with the words 'generation,

choice,' and 'new' at least to show Roger we know what we're doing. There aren't too many ways to combine those words," I continued, "and even if it's only functional, we can still keep working on it while we shoot the spots."

"Gimme an example," said Phil, with more than a hint of skepticism.

"Well, I admit it's not perfect," I ventured, "but how about 'Pepsi — new choices for a new generation.' "

"Allen, it's not that it's not perfect," said Phil. "It *stinks*."

And with that, we both lapsed into silence as we approached the PepsiCo grounds. Then Phil suddenly pulled his car phone off its cradle, punched in a number and asked to speak to Frank Rupp, the head of Pepsi's design department.

"Frank," he said hurriedly, "I need a huge favor. I'm a few minutes away, and we have a big meeting with Roger on the new campaign, and I need someone right away to draw up the theme line we're gonna recommend to Roger. I want him to see it up big, not just typed on a piece of paper. Can you do it? That's great," he continued excitedly after a moment's pause. "It should show the Pepsi logo and right under it, the words should say, 'The choice of a new generation.' "

"Hey, that's not bad," I said to Phil.

"It's not 'not bad.' It really works. It's the line we're gonna sell."

But regardless of how hard Phil sold it, Roger wasn't convinced. He agreed that it did the job, melding the necessary ideas but he thought it had too many words.

"Hang on a minute, Roger," I chimed in, "after the three key words 'choice, new,' and 'generation,' there's only 'the, of,' and 'a' left. That's six words. Lots of theme lines have six words. And as you well know," I added, "even on billboards on major highways, the rule of thumb is that people can understand a line with six words even if they see it for less than a second."

"Okay, okay," said Roger, holding up his hands to fend us off, "since you guys are so hot for it, let me live with it for a couple of days and we'll see."

A few days later, Alan Pottasch, head of advertising at Pepsi, called and told us Roger had approved the line, no doubt heavily influenced by Alan, who liked it as much as we did. A few years later, we all confessed to Roger that it was a last minute, last ditch idea, and told him the story of how it came about. And many years after that, Roger admitted if he had known that at the time, he wouldn't have bought it.

"No way," he said, shaking his head, "not in a million generations."

Pelé 1, Puccini 0

At one time, Bruce Crawford, who ran BBDO before me and Omnicom after me, frequented Lutèce, a famous French restaurant where he had a regular table in the more fashionable front room of the establishment. He rated a level of personal service that went well beyond the captain or even the maître d' attending to him. The owner and chef, André Soltner, would come out from the kitchen to greet Bruce and his guests, chat about business, describe his special dishes for the day, and make recommendations as to what they might particularly enjoy.

Royalty would not have received greater notice than Bruce in Lutèce. This was due not only to his standing in the advertising business, but even more because he ran the Metropolitan Opera, first as its general manager and later as chief executive officer. And beyond the excellence of the food, the wine, the service, and the restaurant's reputation, the treatment afforded Bruce by the management and staff played a major part in the patronage and loyalty he gave them.

One of the reasons for the great success and high standing of Lutèce among the best-known restaurants in New York was the fact that it was a *really* French restaurant, not just a place that happened to have a French menu and wine list.

Soltner was famous among French chefs, the staff all came from France, and the continental décor added to an ambience that made you feel, after only a few minutes at your table, that you were actually dining in Paris.

One evening, Bruce had invited me to join him at Lutèce for dinner with Bernard Brochand, the international head of DDB, another Omnicom advertising agency. Bernard was French, lived in Paris, and was quite entrenched in the social, political, and "old school" network of insiders who control most of the business relationships in that country. He was so well connected, that when he later retired from DDB, he was elected mayor of Cannes, won a seat in the National Assembly, and to this day is an advisor to Jacques Chirac and various ministers with powerful positions in government.

But when we sat down to dinner with Bernard that evening, neither Bruce nor I knew that he was also president of France's premier soccer team, Paris St. Germain, at that time one of the world's most renowned and successful organizations in the game. And given the fact that soccer ("football" as it's known everywhere outside the U.S.) is by far the most popular sport on the globe, engendering in almost every country ferocious loyalties for their national teams, Bernard's position as head of PSG was a far greater claim to fame than any of his business or political positions.

After the usual banter about the state of the opera between Bruce and the various members of the staff who stopped at our table to acknowledge his presence, the waiter who was offering us choices from the selection of breads and dinner rolls noticed a PSG team pin in the lapel of Bernard's jacket.

"Excuse me, sir, but you are from Paris?" he asked Bernard, very tentatively, and in heavily accented English.

"Yes, that's right," he answered in French, which for the rest of the evening became the language spoken between Bernard and the Lutèce staff.

"And you are a follower of Paris St. Germain?" the waiter asked more confidently, now in French.

"Well, in fact, I am the president of the team," declared Bernard in a modest but obviously proud manner.

The waiter's eyes widened in absolute amazement. He turned to another waiter exclaiming, "This gentleman is the president of PSG. Can you believe it? The president of Paris St. Germain!"

"Really? Is it true?" said a second waiter, both now hovering on either side of Bernard.

"Yes, it's true," replied Bernard, just becoming aware of, and somewhat concerned by, the growing commotion around him. More waiters, having somehow been signaled, made their way toward our table. A couple of them pushed their order pads and pens toward Bernard for autographs. Others asked excitedly about the players and the team. The exceptional decorum the staff had been trained to observe evaporated in a frenzy of French football exuberance.

All the while, Bruce, accustomed to the constant attention of the staff, looked on in a state somewhere between surprise and shock, virtually ignored no doubt for the first time in any restaurant, much less his beloved Lutèce. A lesser or petty man governed only by his ego might have gotten angry. But when Bruce saw me look over at him, his expression of astonishment softened. He finally offered an appropriately Gallic shrug and a rueful smile, seeming to acknowledge that opera was no match for football.

So for that evening, even as he sat at it, Monsieur Crawford's table belonged to someone else.

The Baron

Shortly after BBDO, Doyle Dane Bernbach, and Needham Harper formed Omnicom and I became its first chief executive, I began a series of trips to familiarize myself with the agencies of DDB and Needham, which were merging into a new, single entity. One visit was to the German agency of DDB in Düsseldorf, soon to incorporate the smaller unit of Needham in the same city.

The head of the agency was Nicolai von Dellingshausen, a tall, slim, distinguished looking man, whose aristocratic bearing, I quickly learned, was no affectation. He was, in fact, a Baron, with a documented lineage tracing back through generations of German nobility. And as though he needed further credibility, he also pointed out to me, with obvious pride, that he was a cousin of Wernher von Braun, the scientist who headed the development of the V-2 rocket used by Hitler to rain bombs on London. Von Braun's fame increased considerably after World War II, when he came to America to lend his knowledge and expertise to improving our newly growing arsenal of intercontinental ballistic missiles. I must assume it was that part of von Braun's résumé that Nicolai thought would impress me, as opposed to any contribution cousin Wernher might have made on behalf of the Third Reich.

In any event, Nicolai was an accomplished businessman and, as I learned later, a philanthropist of considerable dedication and generosity, whose good works benefited many less fortunate people. He treated me with gentlemanly courtesy, as well as the deference consistent with hosting, if not a higher order of royalty, at least a new boss. He showed me around the DDB agency, introducing me to his various department heads who later joined him in a presentation of the company's history, resources, advertising programs for its clients, and financial performance.

But it was apparent to me that the information was, in fact, quite superficial. Everything they showed required no particular elaboration and could have simply been sent to me in New York. It seemed to me that Nicolai and his staff expressly avoided exposing me to any internal or client issues of disagreement or controversy, which even a novice in the business would know had to exist. It was as though he intended me to see an agency working in perfect harmony and did not want me to know about whatever human or business conflicts existed, however inevitable they might be. And on the few occasions when I saw the opportunity, just based on my own experience in similar situations, to suggest or ask about the possibility of a problem, they were quick to deflect it by assuring me it didn't exist or was not a serious concern.

It therefore became obvious to me that as hospitable as Nicolai was, his ultimate goal was to get me in and out of the agency as quickly, and with as little knowledge of any details of their operations, as possible.

I had arranged my schedule so that Düsseldorf was my last stop in Europe and the visit to DDB my last appointment, so that my flight back to New York would follow the conclusion of Nicolai's presentation. If I had any doubts about his desire to see me on my way, they were completely dispelled by what followed.

"I shall drive you to the airport," said Nicolai, in his

perfect and nearly unaccented English, as I shook hands and said goodbye to his colleagues.

"Really, Nicolai," I responded, "that's good of you but quite unnecessary. Your agency car or a cab will be fine."

"I absolutely insist," he said with a charming smile, as he picked up my suitcase. "I am taking Mr. Rosenshine to his flight," he announced to the receptionist, guiding me toward the elevators. "Please let my assistant know."

"Honestly, Nicolai, I'm sure you have more important things to attend to," I said, resisting the temptation to add, *although I can't imagine what they could be based on the Panglossian "best-of-all-possible-worlds" presentation you just made.*

"There is nothing that cannot wait," he replied with a gallant wave of his arm.

And so Nicolai drove me to the airport. As we pulled up to the Lufthansa entrance, I thanked him for the visit, for his personal attention, and I bade him goodbye.

"No, no," he replied, "I shall park the car and accompany you inside."

"Don't be silly, Nicolai," I said. "I have my ticket, I've reconfirmed the flight, and I'm sure there will be no problem."

"I insist," he insisted once again.

After checking my bag and receiving my boarding pass, along with a card to admit me to the Lufthansa lounge, I reached to shake Nicolai's hand. "Thank you again," I said. "I hope to see you soon."

"No, please, I'll be happy to wait with you for your flight and see you through passport control," said Nicolai.

"Nicolai, I want to make you a promise," I said.

"I don't understand," he replied.

"My promise is," I said, placing my hand over my heart, "I am getting on this plane, I am leaving Germany, and I am going back to New York. Really, I am."

"Well then, *auf wiedersehn*," he said, his bearing visibly

straightening, heels not quite clicking as he turned on them and walked away.

And I kept my word, having learned a good lesson in how subsidiaries report to owner management. Contrary to the popular saying, less is not more. It's all you're going to get.

Bowling for Billings

Every year, the primary trade group of the advertising business, the American Association of Advertising Agencies, holds a convention of its members, usually at a resort hotel. In years past, the Greenbriar in West Virginia, a formal and stately venue with an ambience of southern hospitality served as the traditional gathering place.

At one of these meetings, our client, Lee Iacocca, then chief executive of Chrysler and a world-renowned figure for his success in bring the company back from the brink of bankruptcy, had agreed to make the keynote address. For the organization, Lee provided a major drawing card to insure a high level of attendance. For Lee, a day or two at the Greenbriar would mix a little business with some time for relaxation. And for BBDO, as a member of the association, our attendance would offer us some valuable time with Lee to help build our relationship with him without the accompanying stress of a business meeting in his Detroit headquarters, where every question, comment, or decision could dramatically affect our welfare.

Lee was suitably ensconced in one of the resort's few private villas, and on the night before his speech, he hosted a dinner there for the BBDO people attending the convention. Included in our group were a few wives who had come along to take advantage of the mini-vacation that a couple of days at the Greenbriar afforded. My wife, Missy, was among them, and her propensity for saying what she thought without much concern for the impact her opinions might have on others, would keep me in a state of high anxiety throughout the evening. I remembered a prior dinner with Lee just after the introduction of the Chrysler Minivan, at the time a revolutionary new concept combining the comfort of a car with the capacity of a small truck. More than any other event, this vehicle would likely determine the future of Chrysler and Lee's leadership of the company. Before I knew it, Missy was commenting on the minivan's design.

"I like it," she declared.

So far, so good, I figured.

"Of course, I should like it," Missy continued, "since it's obviously made for women."

Uh, oh, I thought, *here's Chrysler with an image that's the essence of masculinity, and she's telling Lee Iacocca that their breakthrough new product is supposed to be for women?* But before I could think of anything to say that might mitigate Missy's pronouncement, Lee responded, his eyes narrowed and his face set in a look of pure determination.

"Damn *right* it is," he said. "It's everything a family could get in a station wagon but with a helluva lot more space," Lee went on enthusiastically, his salesman's nature taking over. "And you can configure it all kinds of ways for kids or cargo. Women are gonna love it!" he declared triumphantly.

Despite the fact that this hadn't been the first time that Missy's instinct and intuition proved more facile and accurate than my reasoning, just remembering that moment of my insecurity was enough to keep me wary throughout our dinner. But by the time dessert and coffee had been served, and our ongoing consumption of drinks and wine had reached the cognac and liqueur stage, I felt fairly confident that the likelihood of some major faux pas had become remote.

245

Until Lee took a sip of his drink, puffed on his cigar, and said, "Well, what are we gonna do now?"

"I've got a great idea," shot back Missy as I groaned inwardly. "Let's go *bowling!*"

What? I screamed to myself. *Where the hell did that come from?* "Uh, Missy, it's like after midnight and I'm sure the town's bowling alley is closed," I said somewhat tentatively so as not to appear as horrified as I felt at my wife's suggestion that we take America's best-known businessman, not to mention our highest billing client, bowling in the middle of the night.

"I wouldn't take Lee to some local dump," she answered scornfully and with far greater understanding than I had of Lee's sensibility. "This place has its own alley and I'm sure if we call the manager and tell him Lee would like to take his group bowling, they'll open it for us."

"Sounds good to me," said Lee.

And so it was. We left our after-dinner drinks behind, and trooped over to the bowling alley in the basement of the main building, where we found a cooler fully stocked with cold beers, which we passed around as Missy organized us into teams. I doubt anyone broke a hundred, but in fact, no one really kept score. We were too busy hooting at each other's gutter balls and cheering derisively on the rare occasion of a strike or spare. And for the next hour, the camaraderie we had hoped to build between Lee and BBDO could not have been better.

During all the years that Lee was our client, Tom Clark ran our agency in Detroit and spent far more time than anyone else in BBDO with Lee in servicing the Chrysler account. But somehow, I suspect it was Tom's wife, Karen, who understood Lee better than any of us.

And I'm sure my relationship with many BBDO clients could have been a lot easier if I had more often gotten out of Missy's way.

What's in a Name?

In many professional service businesses, the relationship between the companies and their clients often depends in large measure on the credentials, reputations, and past performances of the individuals who deal directly with the clients. It is practically impossible for a layperson to critically evaluate a doctor's diagnosis, a lawyer's brief, an accountant's filing, or an agency's recommendation for an advertising campaign. So when a doctor prescribes a particular treatment, or a lawyer devises a legal strategy, or an accountant tallies up the tax bill, people don't usually argue with them.

In the case of advertising, however, there is a pronounced tendency for client management, even among those who have never been involved in marketing communications, to consider their visceral judgments more relevant than the consumer knowledge and creative insights that they've hired their agencies to provide. It is hard to imagine a client CEO overruling his doctor, lawyer, or personal accountant because he's not happy with what they're telling him. What gives him a considerable level of comfort in all these cases is the trust that comes from knowing his advisors are highly experienced and well regarded in their professions, and have proven track records of success.

But in advertising, even that's not always enough. It sometimes happens that the same CEO will turn down his agency's campaign outright, purely on the subjective basis that he just doesn't like it, regardless of the past accomplishments of the people working on his business.

I had such a client in Rick Donelli (his and the name of the other person in this story are not their own). Rick was in charge of marketing and sales of a major brand of household cleaner, and while he seemed to like us well enough, virtually everything we brought him for the first time on any assignment was subject to skepticism when we presented it, argument when he considered it, and rejection when he grew impatient with discussing it any further. We suffered his constant harangues and harassment because, as is often the case, his brand was one of many that we handled for his company, and resigning it might well have meant losing far more business than just his.

One day, after a typically contentious meeting, Rick seemed to take almost perverse pride in the troubles he well knew he caused us.

"Say, Allen," he said, as I packed up the latest work he had turned down and wanted done over, "tell me the truth. Am I your toughest client?"

"You're close, but you're not the toughest guy I've got to deal with," I replied, taking some pleasure in his obvious disappointment.

"C'mon, who's tougher than me?" he insisted.

"Well, he's not really a client," I said. "He's a personal friend of a big name star we use in one of our other client's campaigns. Nothing happens without this guy's okay. I spend more time negotiating with him than I do on writing the commercials. You're tough, Rick, but he's tougher."

"Whadya say his name was?" asked Rick.

"Oh, you wouldn't know him. His name is Tucci."

"Did you say 'Tucci?' That's not Mario Tucci you're talkin' about?" Rick asked, this time with a look of wariness.

"That's right, Mario Tucci. Do you know him?" I asked.

"No, I never met him," said Rick slowly, then pausing before he continued, his face frowning with seeming concern. "But you're tellin' me you *know* Mario Tucci? You *talk* to him? You *meet* with him?" said Tom, incredulously.

"Yeah, I told you who he is," I said, puzzled by his questions.

"*You have no idea who he is,*" said Rick, spacing his words and slowly shaking his head from side to side as he spoke them.

"Oh, I get it," I said, laughing. "Are you trying to put me on? Are you telling me he's supposed to be 'The Godfather' or something? Nice try, Rick."

"Lemme put it this way, Allen," said Rick, emphasizing each word, "I'm not tellin' you anything."

With that, our conversation ended. He never mentioned Mario Tucci again. And overnight, Rick became one of the most cooperative, complimentary, and considerate clients I ever had.

Somehow, I seemed to have made him an offer he couldn't refuse.

The Later, the Better

Shortly after joining BBDO as a copywriter, I had the opportunity to work with Alphonse Normandia, an art director who would become a legend in the agency. His icon status was due mostly to his longevity since he retired only after working in the agency for almost sixty years. In the last few years before he left, I'd sometimes see him in the elevator or hobbling down the hall on his cane.

"Hiya, chief," he'd invariably say. "How are we doin'?"

"Okay, Al, how are *you* doing?" would be my usual reply.

"Can't complain, chief," he'd answer. "I'm still in there kickin'."

In fact, Alphonse's artistic talent, wit, common sense, and good nature during all these years would each have deserved just as much notice and respect as his exceptionally long career in the business.

In addition to his ability to design the visual structure of commercials, Alphonse had a uniquely expressive artistic style, using cartoon drawings instead of realistic renderings. He was thus able to capture the emotional sense of how a character was intended to look and act, particularly in scenes that called for comedic or exaggerated portrayals. In fact, beyond his work in advertising, Alphonse was a successful cartoonist,

250

creating many hilarious drawings and captions for a variety of magazines.

He was also something of a practical joker, at least two of his pranks becoming part of BBDO lore. Alphonse had the look and features of the quintessential Italian shopkeeper — short, stocky, prematurely balding, with glasses perched on a Roman nose above a handlebar moustache. He actually looked like the plastic glasses, rubber nose, and attached moustache you could buy in a novelty shop and wear as a funny disguise. Which is exactly what he did to interview a young, unsuspecting artist looking to land a job at the agency. When the hopeful candidate opened the door to Alphonse's office and saw what he was wearing on his face, he laughed accommodatingly.

"You look funny in that get-up," he said.

"Really?" responded Alphonse, removing it to reveal practically the same face, but this time, his real one. No one ever asked how the rest of the interview went.

A more elaborate joke resulted from BBDO's location for many years directly across the street from the Roosevelt Hotel. At night, voyeurism became something of an agency sport. People working late would take shifts scanning the windows of the hotel rooms, hoping to catch someone in a compromising situation and calling in the troops whenever they did. But when Alphonse watched, he had a layout of the hotel he had made, noting the numbers of the rooms facing the agency. And whenever he saw someone doing something that should have been done behind closed curtains, he'd grab the phone.

"This is God speaking," he'd announce to the horrified hotel guest. "You should be ashamed of yourself."

I never got to know Alphonse as a friend outside the office. But I did have some idea that as reasoned, as calm, and as unflappable as he was even during the most chaotic client crisis, his personal life was far less tranquil and not at all under control. My first hint that he lived more peacefully in the office than at home came after I had become creative director of the agency, essentially Alphonse's boss. One evening, as almost the entire creative department worked into the late hours on a major client presentation scheduled that week, I got a very unusual phone call.

"Is this Allen Rosenshine?" asked a female voice I didn't recognize.

"Yes, who's this?"

"This is Alphonse Normandia's wife," she responded testily, "and I want to know where the little bastard is."

"Excuse me?" was about all I could think to say.

"He told me he's working late but I know he's lying," she exclaimed. "I just called his number and there's no answer."

"Well, I can assure you he's here," I told her. "Do you want me to find him and have him call you back."

"No, you're lying too," she shot back, and hung up.

I found Alphone and told him about the call. He just shook his head sadly. "Yeah, that was her, all right," was all he said.

Years later, I got my second inkling that all had not been bliss in the Normandia household. After Alphonse eventually moved out, a mutual friend told me that for the last ten years of his marriage, he had lived in the basement of his house. I didn't ask whether he had visitation rights to come upstairs to see his children.

In my early years at the agency, Alphonse gave me two very insightful and valuable pieces of advice that I used to good advantage in getting my work recognized by the company's management. He told me that Jim Jordan, who ran the creative department of the agency, would often prowl the offices late at night, looking on the desks of the writers and art directors to see what they were working on. Occasionally, when I wanted to be sure he'd see a particular idea for a campaign that my supervisor or perhaps some account executive had rejected, I'd leave the layout right on top of my desk or prominently displayed on the wall where Jim couldn't miss it.

Assuming he liked it, the next morning I'd get a call from him asking why he hadn't seen it, which I'd dutifully report to whoever had turned it down. Of course, I could truthfully deny ever showing it to him, while playing dumb as to how he found out about it.

But the shrewdest tactic Alphonse taught me was that whenever we had a creative "gang bang" going on (everyone in every creative group, all trying to think up a new campaign for a client or new business prospect), if I had an idea I thought might really impress our management, I should never show it until the last minute.

"Lock it in your desk and forget it," he said. "Don't let anyone see it until the day before the client meeting and then tell the big guy you just came up with it. By then, the whole place will be in a total panic and if your idea is even half good, he'll jump on it. Remember," he said, "heroes never save the day until the last minute."

It didn't always work but even then, at least it showed you stayed in the game until time ran out. Which was how Alphonse played it until he finally retired, when neither his indomitable spirit nor his cane could keep him going any longer.

The Publicity Stunt

When BBDO advertised Lucky Strike cigarettes and Schaefer Beer, creating commercials for the broadcasts of Brooklyn Dodger baseball games, the clients were always concerned with how the team played, since they benefited when the Dodgers were winning and their fans followed the games with greater enthusiasm. The clients also had a stake in the Dodger players themselves as de facto endorsers of their products, so that any kind of negative publicity involving a player became a problem the agency had to handle.

This was the case with one of the Dodger pitchers, Billy Loes, a particularly newsworthy player among the New York sports writers since he was born and raised in the city. As a result, while he was hardly a source of baseball wit or wisdom, he got more coverage in the press than many of his teammates.

So when a young lady from his old haunts accused him of getting her pregnant, the papers broke the story with big, bold headlines. While today, a paternity suit would hardly cause much of a stir and could be quickly dealt with using DNA evidence, back when the Dodgers still played in Brooklyn, it would be the basis for continuing coverage in the sports news and a source of trouble for the clients, the agency, the Dodger organization, and of course, for Loes himself.

At the ballpark, the other Dodger players showed their support of Loes and their sympathy for his public predicament.

"Way t' go, Billy."

"When's the wedding, buddy?"

"I hope the kid can throw harder than you."

"Nice shot of you in the *Post,* kiddo."

"Can she bake a cherry pie, charmin' Billy?" sang a chorus of voices across the locker room.

In fact, Loes was distraught. Since he wasn't married, he didn't have to be concerned with the reaction of a betrayed wife. He had what he considered a far bigger problem.

"What am I gonna tell my mom when she sees this?" he moaned to one of our account executives who worked on the Lucky Strike and Schaefer advertising.

"First of all, Billy, did you do it?" he asked. "Because if there's any doubt you're the father, you could deny it."

"I dunno," Loes answered, "lotsa people know I been out with her and I'd look like a pussy if I said I never laid her. She's just pissed off 'cause I told her I didn't wanna marry her. Christ, my mother's gonna tear my head off."

"Listen, Billy, you've got bigger problems than your mother," said our account man. "You could get suspended from the team."

"I'm tellin' ya," Loes went on, "my old lady's gonna kill me."

"You're not listening, Billy. If you don't settle this thing with your girlfriend one way or another, you could come up on criminal charges."

"How's she gonna face all her friends in the old neighborhood? Oh man," said Loes, nearly in tears, "she's never gonna get over this."

"Look, Billy," said the BBDO representative with growing impatience, "we've got to get you a lawyer and we've gotta sit down and figure out how we're gonna handle the PR on this."

"Yeah, yeah," Loes replied distractedly, "but first I gotta figure out what I'm gonna tell my mom." Then, suddenly his eyes brightened with excitement. "Hey, I got it! I got it!" he exclaimed. "You just said somethin' about PR, right?

"That's right," the account executive replied, hopeful that Loes was beginning to appreciate the real scope of the problem. "The team, and our client, and probably you will have to say something to the press."

"Yeah, man, that's the answer," said Loes, smiling with relief.

"What the hell are you talking about, Billy?" said our account man, becoming exasperated again.

"I just figured it out. I know how I'm gonna explain this to my mom," said Loes, triumphantly. "I'm gonna tell her it's a *publicity stunt*."

I knew my mother always loved me no matter how stupid the things I said or did. In the end, Mrs. Loes was no different.

Mind Over Money

After Pepsi-Cola had run a breakthrough campaign in the mid-'80s featuring Michael Jackson, the question became what to do for an encore. We understood that we could not replicate the advertising drama or the attendant publicity generated when Michael appeared in our commercials. Having established the obviously successful strategy of linking Pepsi with the cutting edge of the music scene, we looked for a suitable singing star with the kind of popularity and success that could continue what had begun with Michael.

We set our sights on Lionel Richie, whose song, "All Night Long," was right up there with Michael's hits at the top of the charts. After confirming Lionel's interest in doing commercials for Pepsi, we made our way to the Hollywood office of his manager, Ken Kragen, to discuss the possibilities.

Kragen did not typify the cliché Hollywood agent. He didn't dress ostentatiously, flaunt the size of his deals, drop the names on his Rolodex, or display other cues of his stature. He didn't play any of the power games that we ordinarily had to put up with from most of the people who represent the stars in the Hollywood galaxy. He was a laid back, clear thinking, articulate businessman who also guided the career and managed the assets of Kenny Rogers, at that time probably the most successful of all the country and western singers. Kragen's understanding of how to market Lionel was evident from his very first questions.

"What's Pepsi's marketing strategy and how does Lionel fit in?" he asked. "Why would you want him instead of, for example, Kenny?"

"The idea is for Pepsi to distinguish and differentiate itself from Coke by associating the brand with whatever and whoever stands for what's young and hip and cool." I answered. "We give Coke its due as an icon of middle-American, middle-age values. They own white picket fences, Sunday dinners, backyard barbecues, baseball, mom, apple pie, and the beer and bon-bon brigade. We want Pepsi to be where the younger generation lives and breathes. Our strategy is to make Pepsi the symbol of their energy, enthusiasm, optimism, and the soft drink for anyone of any age who appreciates, and wants to feel themselves a part of, those youthful attitudes. Kenny Rogers is Coke. Lionel Richie is Pepsi," I concluded.

"Well, that's really interesting," said Kragen. "Because last week, Coke sent their plane out here and flew me to their headquarters in Atlanta to offer us one helluva lot of money for Lionel to do *their* commercials."

That was certainly not welcome news but not really surprising in response to the groundswell of marketing and advertising momentum that Pepsi had generated with Michael. I didn't relish having to report to our client that we had come up with too little, too late to win Lionel for our brand. And worse yet, had lost him to Coke.

"So what are you gonna do?" I asked, fearing the answer.

"I'm thinking about it," he replied, "because I asked them the same question I just asked you."

"What did they say?" I asked Kragen.

"They said Coke is the biggest pop culture brand in the world and if Lionel wants to be number one, he should team up with number one."

"Wouldn't tying Lionel to Coke's older fashioned image damage him with his audience?" I suggested. "And don't you think going with Coke right after Michael went with Pepsi makes Lionel look kind of copycat and maybe even a little desperate?" I ventured, trying not to show Kragen what desperate looked like.

"Yeah, I thought about all that too," said Kragen, "so I asked the Coke guys exactly the same things. You know what they said?"

"No, but I'm dying to find out," I said, fearing there might be some figurative truth to my answer.

"They said they'd pay Lionel more than Michael got from Pepsi and they'd publicize it so everyone would know that Lionel got a bigger deal than Michael," said Kragen, shaking his head and smiling. "They think I'm only looking for more money. They just don't get it."

Happily for us, they didn't get Lionel either. Pepsi did.

It's always good to know that you can still beat a competitor even when they have more money to spend on promoting their product, more clout with the trade, better distribution (Roberto Goizueta, who built Coca-Cola into a symbol of shareholder value once said, "Pepsi can have their great advertising, I've got more trucks."), and an icon brand that sells more in practically every country of the world.

It was also nice to learn that even in La-La Land, the font of rampant ego, inflated beyond reason by Monopoly money, it's possible to do a smart deal with both sides getting a good return on their intentions.

But it's still a long shot. Pepsi beat the odds with both Michael and Lionel. But some years later, the craziness caught up with us.

Madonna got millions to do a Pepsi commercial that you've never seen. Because when she was through trashing religion and good taste in the name of Pepsi, it never ran.

259

The Honeymooners

Within days after Missy and I married in 1979, we attended the first global meeting of BBDO agency managers, which took place at a coastal hotel in the Netherlands. The agency had held numerous regional meetings before, but this was a conference that brought together the top managements of BBDO companies from all regions of the world. It was a historic event in both the worldwide growth of the company and my personal life since it was also the first stop on our honeymoon trip.

While the meeting agenda featured many business issues needing attention, an equally if not more important reason for the gathering was simply for the BBDO managers to get to know each other better. Arguably, the advertising business, more than others, depends on personal relationships not just with clients but also between diverse people within the agency, often from different parts of the world, who must work efficiently together to provide effective communications solutions for the brands we serve. And as multinational companies expanded their businesses around the globe, serving them well demanded increasing levels of cooperation and understanding between our agencies in many countries and cultures. Making that possible meant that within our growing global organization, we had to put faces with names, and build, if not friendships, at least familiarity well beyond what faxes or phones could generate.

Thus, we planned on social events and free time for casual conversations among our managers to break the ice that differences and distances naturally formed between us. And to underline the importance we placed on the personal side of the meeting, we encouraged our people to bring their wives and husbands to help promote the feeling of family that we wanted to develop within the company.

As a result, we learned quite a lot about each other, in some instances more than we expected or needed to know, such as who was reputed, if not proven, to be sleeping with whom, or how some among us underwent major personality changes, both for better and worse, as the alcohol level in our bloodstreams increased.

The highlight of the social side of our agenda was a dinner in a restaurant famous for recreating the atmosphere and style of a medieval inn. Since our group had the entire place to ourselves, instead of the usual layout of many separate tables, the floor plan had been reconfigured to seat all of us on benches on either side of two long wooden tables, very close and parallel to each other. With each new pitcher of wine poured throughout the meal, our tongues, clothing, and other forms of social inhibitions loosened. The quaintness of food served with neither dishes nor silverware, but rather tossed on the table for us to pass and eat with our hands, hastened the breakdown of manners and mores.

Soon, to the accompaniment of an anachronistically contemporary band, our otherwise prim and proper partner from Melbourne, making a show of taking off and flinging away his jacket and tie, climbed on top of his table, pulling his wife up after him as she shed her shoes to dance amidst the remnants of the meal. Our manager from Rome, whom we later learned had an uncle who sang opera at La Scala, cajoled the band into backing his surprisingly good renditions of various arias, which for some reason, he felt compelled to sing stripped to the waist.

For my part, to the astonishment of my new bride, I took Chris Crawford, our chief executive Bruce Crawford's wife, by the hand and to the dance floor, not risking the top of a table, but nevertheless taking some chance with this very dignified, very reserved, and very corporately reticent lady. Fortunately, she seemed to tolerate, if not enjoy, the moment. And having not yet lost all sense of the politically correct, I also paid attention to Bruce, whose well-known commitment to proper attire left him about the only man in the room still in jacket and tie.

"How'd you like to make five hundred bucks in the next few minutes?" I whispered. Bruce looked at me quizzically without answering. "I'll bet ten guys a hundred each that before the evening is over, you'll get out on the dance floor in your shirtsleeves."

"Everybody knows I wouldn't do that."

"That's the point," I said. "That's why they'll take the bet. They'll think I'm drunk, which I am a little, but then all you have to do is *do it,* we split a thousand dollars, and they'll know they've been had." I had depended on the wine and his appreciation of a little scam to overcome his formality. But neither was enough.

"I don't think so," said Bruce, his resolve and his back visibly stiffening.

Regardless, the evening was a complete success in making some strangers colleagues, some colleagues friends, and leaving most everyone with a feeling that BBDO meant something to them beyond just the company where they worked. Even Bruce, jacket buttoned and tie still perfectly knotted, ended the evening with a few of us, our wives having long since departed, as we continued drinking, laughing, and being harmlessly foolish well into the wee hours. We finally closed the restaurant but not before our leader endeared himself further by commandeering more wine for the bus ride back to our hotel.

Missy had put up with all these shenanigans, understanding the need for the company to develop a more collegiate culture and knowing that we would then have time to ourselves on our real honeymoon, driving through France from Paris to Provence, stopping wherever our fancy took us, and ending our trip in St. Paul de Vence, a truly medieval town. It was, in fact, a wonderful week away from the business.

But there was still one unplanned agency event in store for us.

I had arranged for us to have lunch at the Colombe d'Or, perhaps the most famous inn and restaurant in the south of France. A leisurely meal, stretching into the late afternoon, sipping wine on their beautiful terrace overlooking the mountainside on which the town was built centuries before, with a walk through the inn to admire their collection of paintings by Picasso, Matisse, Renoir, and many other French masters of a period we both loved, would put a romantic exclamation point on our honeymoon.

We arrived at the restaurant after a long walk through the town from the authentic medieval inn where we stayed. We were seated at the edge of the terrace where we had a panoramic view of the magnificent terrain. We raised a first glass of champagne to drink to each other and our life together.

"Hey, Al!" I heard someone shout before I had uttered a word of my toast.

As I turned, I saw to my absolute horror a few people from BBDO, a couple of clients, and a film director I recognized, accompanied by about a dozen others from his production company, all being seated just a few tables away from us.

What a disaster, I thought. But it got even worse.

"Why don't you join us?" said the client.

"Oh, shit," I heard Missy murmur.

We then did what advertising people do on their honeymoon. We had lunch with the client.

Cupcakes in the Underpants

Sometimes, you bring a client an advertising idea they just don't know how to deal with. Obviously, that isn't the intent but it just works out that way. The bottom line is that they don't want to produce it, but for some reason, they also don't want to come right out and say so. Perhaps they think they will look uncreative in the eyes of the agency. Or maybe they think they will offend the sensibilities of the writer or art director who thought up the advertising they don't want to run. Whatever the reason, the dialogue can become certifiably insane.

One such commercial called for a teenage girl to try shoplifting an item from a supermarket. As I think we would all admit from experience, stealing some small, inconsequential product from a store is something most kids do just for the thrill of the risk and the childish exultation of getting away with it. (In my case, which I can now safely confess since the statute of limitations expired about half a century ago, I would pilfer a few lead fishing sinkers from a sports store, which my fellow hoodlums and I would hammer into slugs we used in subway turnstiles, thus compounding our criminal offenses.) This was the level of felonious behavior the young girl in our commercial would undertake, to show her bowing to the peer pressure of her friends putting her up to it.

The objective was to have her wind up in an embarrassing, stupid situation, which she would do by trying to walk off with a package of cupcakes in her panties. As the manager of the store approaches her with a suspicious look, the script called for her to describe to the viewer her growing panic.

"I've got two chocolate cupcakes with chocolate frosting in my underpants," she would say, adding ruefully, "and they don't want to stay there."

The client didn't doubt that this situation led directly to the message they wished to convey, which incidentally had nothing to do with cupcakes. They were not even in the food business. But they expressed a concern about our describing the cupcakes as being in the girl's underpants. Actually, they worried more about the use of the word "underpants" than the act itself. This was quickly dealt with by changing it to her pants instead. And at the end of the meeting, the agency went home happy, thinking the commercial had been approved.

Not quite.

The next day, an e-mail came from the client. Because there is no way to summarize, paraphrase, reconstruct, or otherwise reproduce their comments, what follows is verbatim:

We can live with pants. However, the image of two chocolate cupcakes is giving us trouble. We are saying that one or three would be different in imagery than two. Also, frosted cupcakes are different than chocolate cupcakes with chocolate frosting. Unfortunately, vanilla, strawberry, or white frosting all have similar problems.

I would love to have been the proverbial fly on the wall during whatever discussion resulted in that message. It would have been hilarious if only it didn't hurt too much to laugh. Our instinctive thought was, *What the hell are they talking about?* Of course, we translated this to a more client correct response, suggesting that we were not quite sure what they meant, so we hoped they'd discuss it further. But that was the only hope I had. I was sure that in the next meeting, the cupcakes would be killed.

But oh, me of little faith. I was wrong. For reasons no one tried to explain, nor would I understand, we were forced to make *Sophie's Choice.*

One of the cupcakes survived.

Afterword

This is more a last story than an afterword. I tell it here because as the stories go, this one is not as advertised. It has nothing whatever to do with the ad game or anyone connected with it. It's about a different game and it's only about me, a few years before I got into the business. But somehow, it's perhaps a precursor of the kinds of things that lay in store for me, many of which I've written about in this book.

It happened during my junior year at Columbia University. When I got there, I had no idea what I wanted to do with my life, which in today's milieu would be no problem. But back then, it was a source of considerable anxiety. You were expected to declare your major course of study early on, preferably even when you applied for admission to college. And having come from Stuyvesant High School in New York, where the importance of math, physics, and chemistry far outweighed anything resembling a liberal art, I entered Columbia as a pre-chemical engineering student. That commitment lasted less than two years since the one thing I learned for sure during that time was that I had no interest whatsoever in the subject.

But I did have something to which I dedicated myself completely — becoming a member of the varsity basketball team. To this day, I can't explain why that possessed me. But it did. And it was no easy task. While I played a pretty good game in the schoolyards, I had never played basketball on a regular team, having not grown to my six-foot height until my freshman year in college.

Perhaps I was taken with the fact that Columbia's star player was Chet Forte, who at five feet, six inches tall was nevertheless an All-American, recognized as one of the best college players in the country. And if Forte's fame was not enough, Columbia's basketball coach, Lou Rossini, also had a national reputation, having guided the team to successes rarely achieved by an Ivy League school in post-season NCAA tournaments.

In any event, I came to Columbia focused on the day that tryouts would begin for the basketball program. My first step was to try and make the freshman team. In those days, freshmen were not allowed to play varsity ball, but being on the "frosh" squad was essential to any hope of ever moving up to the varsity. And for a "walk on" player (one who had never been approached or scouted for the basketball team, and whom the coaches had never heard of), I did pretty well. The practices were conducted by Rossini himself, and I survived the first few cuts in which the squad was reduced in number.

I felt my chances improve with each of the few encouraging comments Rossini directed to me personally, the most memorable being when I was playing against a guy much taller than me, a player specifically recruited from a top Ohio high school team.

"Jesus Christ," screamed Rossini at the kid, "that guy's half your size, he never played high school ball, and he's beatin' the shit outta you."

As fate or Rossini would have it, I didn't beat quite enough of it out of him, since he made the team and I didn't. I was relegated to the "B" squad. But because that team was an integral part of the program, I felt I had done reasonably well.

I was one of the five starters and was invited to the pre-season varsity practices during my second year.

Again I thought I kept up well enough with guys who had far more experience — not to mention natural talent — than I, but as the squad was progressively trimmed down, I eventually got cut. But one of the assistant coaches told me Rossini wanted me to play on the junior varsity team.

Okay, I thought, *it's not the varsity but if Rossini wants me there, that's still a pretty good sign.*

So I played JV basketball during my sophomore year, after which I was again asked to join the varsity practices the following season. By now, I assumed I was better known and certainly had more experience in the program than any recruited player coming from the freshman team, and therefore stood a good chance of finally making the varsity, despite being a junior with only two years of playing eligibility remaining.

But I was wrong. I found myself again on the JV team.

This time, I gave considerable thought to whether I had any hope at all of ever wearing the varsity uniform. I had no illusions of ever playing very much, if at all, in actual games. But I still had the albeit fading hope of being asked to fill in, for example, in case someone got hurt, or whatever.

So I played for the JV team again. Then, at mid-season, "whatever" happened — three varsity players were put on academic probation for low grades in the fall semester and could not play for the second half of the schedule.

This was it, I thought. It was the break I'd been playing and praying for. And sure enough, at the next JV game, Rossini came in person to watch us play, something he hadn't done even once in all the time I had been on the team. I was certain he had only one purpose in mind — to pick one or two of us to join the varsity for the rest of the season.

With visions of my dream dancing in my head and doses of extra adrenalin pumping through my veins, I played the game of my life. I was high scorer with twenty-four points. I

269

took rebounds, got assists and made steals, all in front of Rossini, whom I could see with well-timed glances, taking notes.

Then, when the final buzzer sounded, I watched through the corners of my eyes as Rossini moved to the doorway that led off the court, no doubt I thought, positioning himself to say something to whomever he had selected for the varsity team. I timed my exit so that I'd be the last one off the court, thinking it would be easier that way for Rossini to talk to me privately. With my towel draped around my neck and my head lowered modestly, eyes on the floor, I walked past him, expecting the tap on my shoulder.

He tapped. I turned. He looked me straight in the eyes and smiled as he reached out to give me an approving punch on my arm.

"Nice game, Shineberg," he said, as he turned and walked away.

So did I. I never played another minute of basketball for Columbia.

Years later, it occurred to me that if I ever wrote an auto-biography, Rossini's final words to me would make a good title. But I tell the story here because I will never write that other book. My life is really my family, which is nobody else's business. And as for my business, you've just read the most interesting parts of it.

The rest I have no wish to relive, least of all to write a how-to-succeed-in-advertising book. I think I've already of-fered the best advice I can:

Don't lose your sense of humor. You'll need it.

Acknowledgments

I dedicated this book to my family, my true life and legacy. There are others I want to acknowledge as well:

Bruce Crawford, for his decades of friendship and faith in me, without which I can't imagine where I would have ended up;

Phil Dusenberry, my partner for many years, whose extraordinary creative talent made my leadership at BBDO meaningful;

Andrew Robertson, whose intelligence, leadership, and energy allowed me to leave BBDO in the hands of someone who will surely take it farther than I;

Tom Dillon and Jim Jordan, who helped me up the first rungs of the corporate ladder;

Willi Schalk and Keith Reinhard, who as much as anyone, made Omnicom happen;

John Wren, who along with Bruce, made it a great success;

Susan McAleer and Pat Deal before her, executive assistants without whom I would have spent my days with little idea of what I was supposed to do next;

The innumerable people of BBDO around the world who made me proud to be a part of it;

The many clients of BBDO without whom there would be nothing to say, especially the people at PepsiCo and Gillette, to whom circumstances kept me closer for longer than any others;

Arnold Levenstein, who ran a small industrial agency and gave me my start in advertising;

Larry Berger, former head of TV production at BBDO, who got me into the agency.

And the many others I owe, far beyond any brief expression of thanks.

Index

273